Dear Readers,

It is with grateful hearts that we Thank all of our subscribers for your support of our new venture. It is our goal to represent the many artists in the industry with a focus on the Members of the Professional Doll Makers Art Guild during our first year.

We are always looking for submissions. Artists who have new works they would like to share, articles they would like to write, tutorials they would like to share are always welcome. We will be doing a Teacher's Section in a future issue and would like to hear from all doll makers who either teach online or in person and what types of dolls you make. Teaching the next generation of doll artists is very important to our industry. We want to promote all artists who teach, so lets hear from you. Contact us via internationaldollartists@gmail.com

We are here to do that for you and intend to keep everyone informed and up-to-date with tutorials, tips of the trade and new and upcoming inventive and exciting art. We're pleased to present to you our first issue of the exciting and new **IDA MAGAZINE!**

Subscribe by visiting our website.

internationaldollartists.com

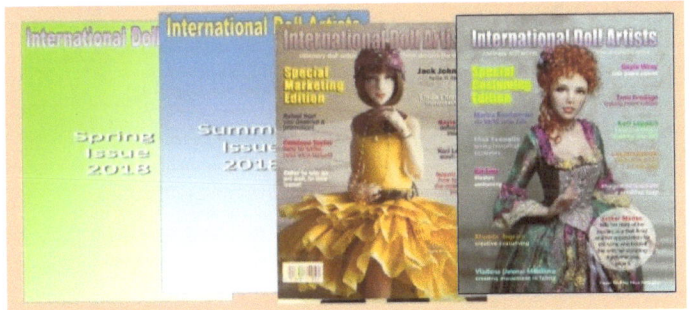

Copyright © 2017 by Cherie Fretto. All rights reserved. No part of this publication may be reproduced, distributed, or transmitted in any form or by any means, including photocopying, recording, or other electronic or mechanical methods, without the prior written permission of the publisher, except in the case of brief quotations embodied in critical reviews and certain other noncommercial uses permitted by copyright law. For permission requests, write to the publisher, addressed "Attention: Creative Director," at the email address below. Publisher is not responsible for unsolicited materials. Product names used are used with permission of the copyright and trademark holders, for editorial use only. No further rights are implied. All subscriptions are by download only. With printed copies on demand. Delivery will be 4 times a year as stated on our website. An email will be delivered to notify you of accessibility.

IDA Publishing ©
internationaldollartists@gmail.com
www.internationaldollartists.com
Published and printed in the USA.

Who is IDA Magazine?

Cherie Fretto: Publisher /Editor in Chief

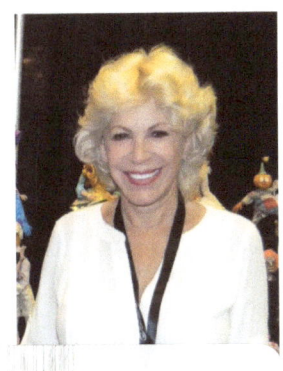

Cherie is the President and CEO of the Professional Doll Makers Art Guild. She's received many Diamond Awards for her OOAK polymer clay dolls, but specializes in BJDs, where she does her own molding and casting for limited editions.

www.BJDStudio.com

Linda Ehrenfried: Managing Editor/Creative Director

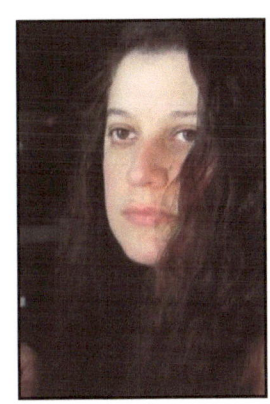

Linda is the Executive VP of the Professional Doll Makers Art Guild. She is the webmaster and runs the day-to-day operations of the Guild and the apprentice program. She's a master artist of OOAK dolls in polymer clay, paper clay and mixed media.

www.charmcityoriginals.com

Gayle Wray, Editor/Graphic Designer

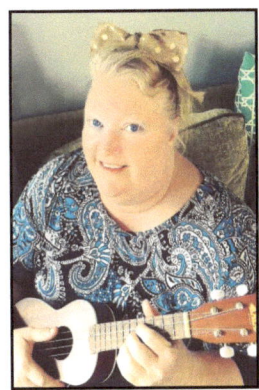

Gayle is an award-winning artist and graphic designer, author, and master cloth doll artist. She's the recipient of the Light Space & Time solo-artist showcase winner and her dolls have been featured at the Ontario Museum of History & Art.

www.gaylewray.com

International Doll Artists - January 2018

Special Costuming Edition
Featured Articles

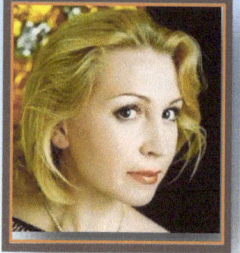

Marina Bondarenko
"My 50/50 Color Rule"
Page 10

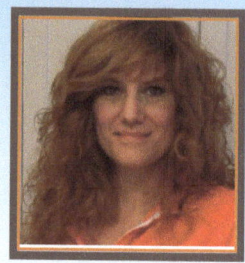

Elisa Fenoglio
"Loving Historical Costumes"
Page 52

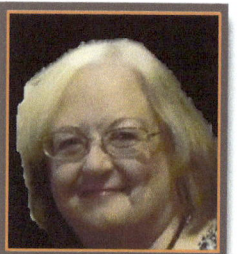

Kat Lees
"Illusion Costuming"
Page 18

Rhonda Ingram
"Creative Costuming"
Page 56

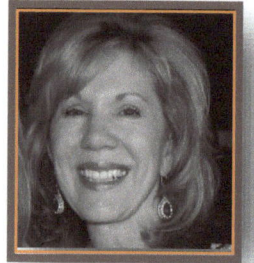

Marguerite Noschese
A Creative Leap"
Page 22

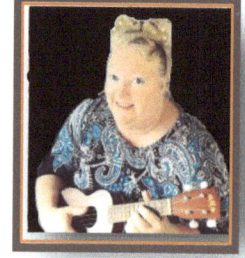

Gayle Wray
"A Creative Leap"
Page 60

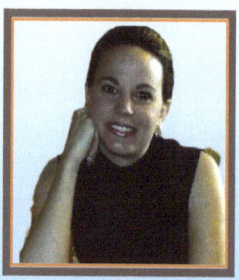

Kori Leppart
"Show your work"
Page 34

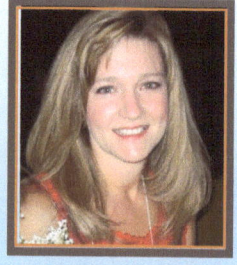

Tami Eveslage
"Making Moira's Shoes"
Page 66

What's Inside

My Journey as a Doll Artist

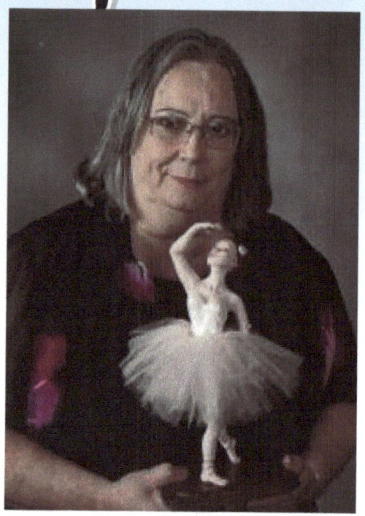

Esther Manso tells her story of her journey as a Doll Artist and her appreciation for everyone who helped her with her sculpting in polymer clay.

Page 6

Quarterly Quote:

The aim of art is to represent not the outward appearance of things, but their inward significance.

Artistotle

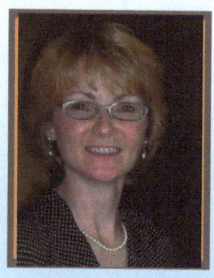

Lisa Wroblewski
"Costuming out of the box"
Page 38

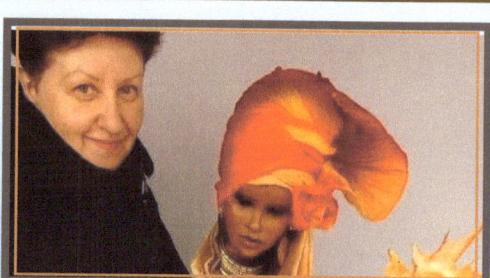

Creating movement in Fabric
By Vladlena (Jelena) Mihailova
Page 28

Special Costuming Edition

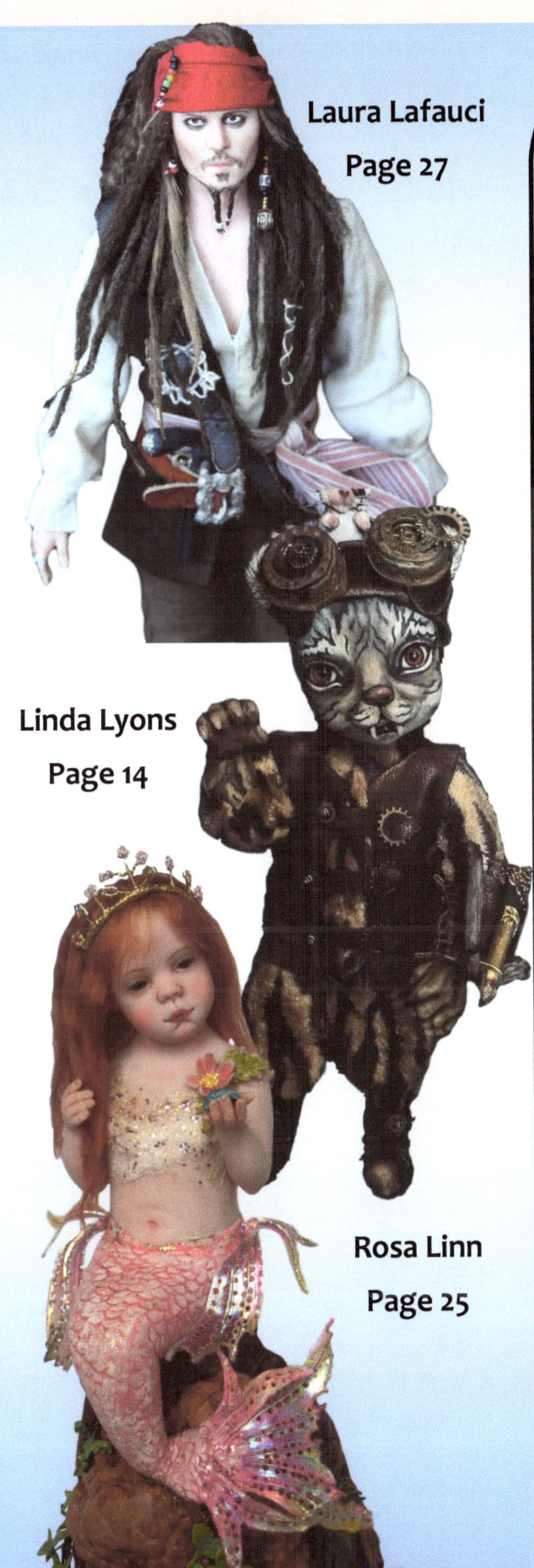

Laura Lafauci
Page 27

Linda Lyons
Page 14

Rosa Linn
Page 25

Artist Voices

Esther Manso 6

Alessandra Nicolin............9

Michelle Albert...............21

Alicia Wilkinson...............32

Hajnalka Mayor..............36

Natasha Nazarova 42

Ioanna Paraskeva............44

Deborah Randall.............48

Leslie Duthie..................50

Sue McMahon...............55

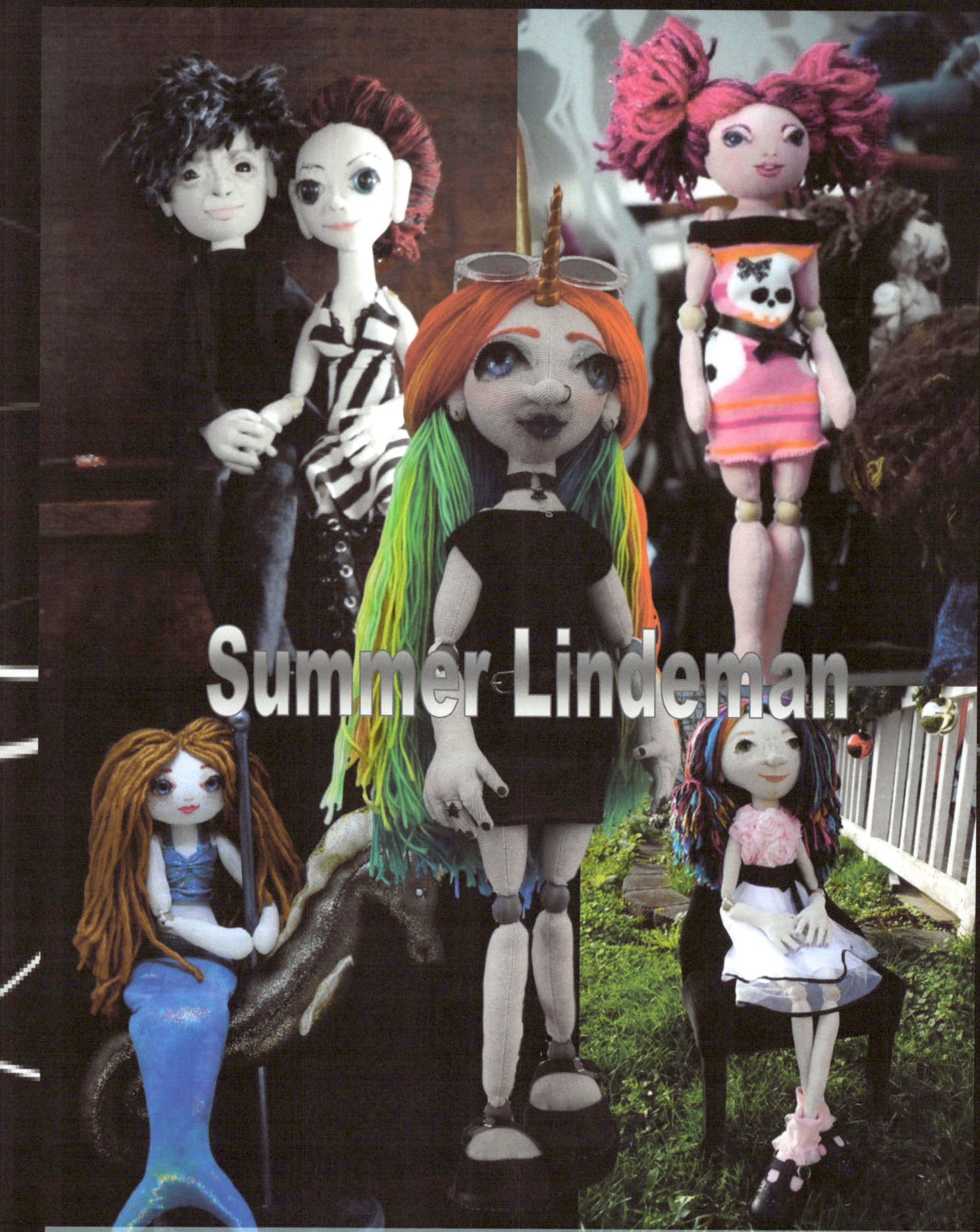

Summer Lindeman, Little Bea Imaginings, specializing in cloth dolls & toys, handmade, one of a kind at www.littlebea.com or facebook.com/LittleBeaImagining

Michelle Collins

Works with Portrait Sculpting

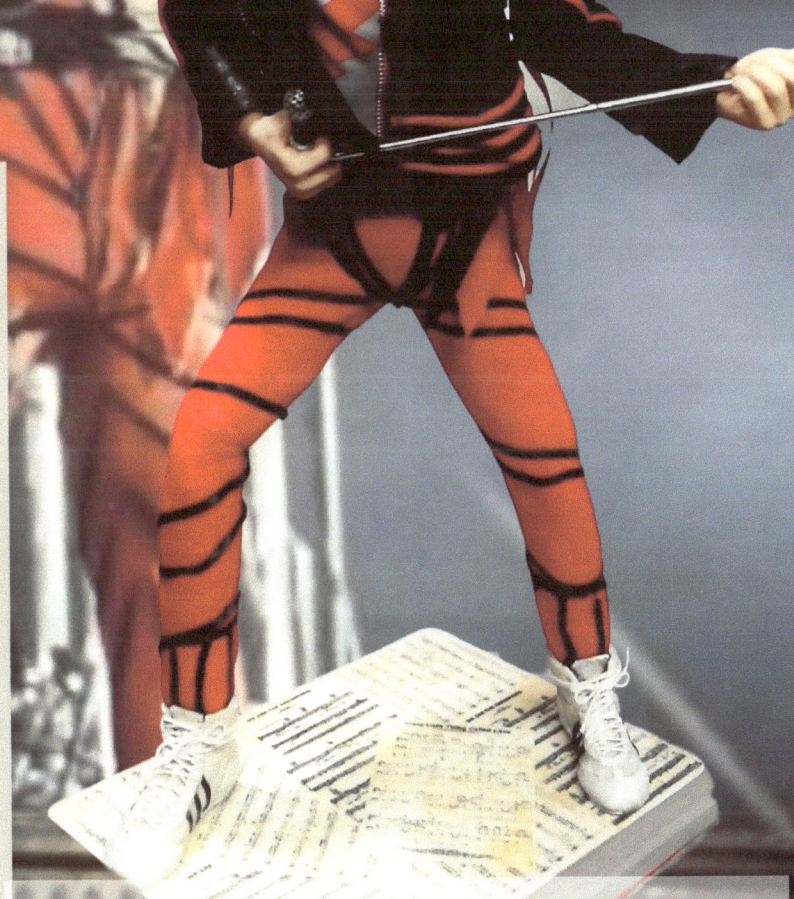

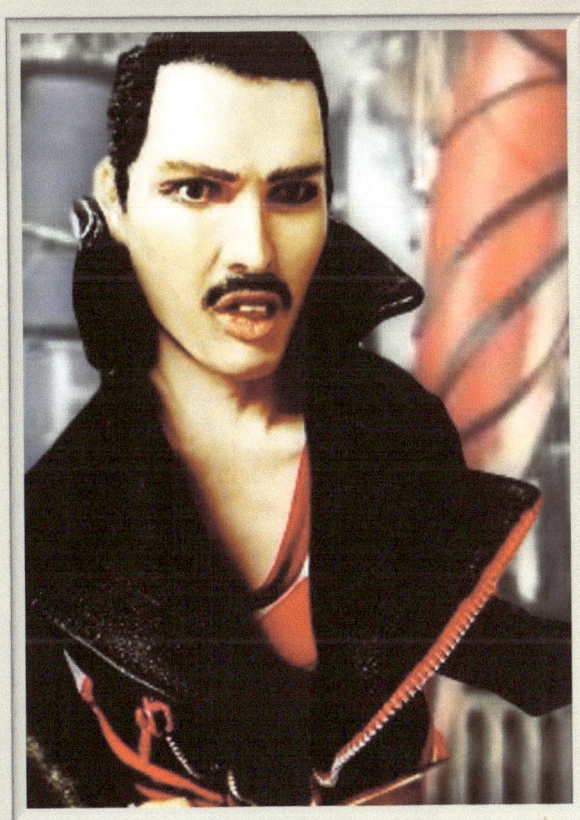

Inspiration Freddie Mercury from a live performance for Live Aid at Wembley Stadium in 1985

Collins Toy Emporium

mcdbookseller@gmail.com

My Journey as a Doll Artist

In 2010 after having to quit working due to a serious illness I found myself with a lot of time of my hands. Not wanting to fall into a deep dark hole of depression I went looking for something that would fill my soul and keep me busy. I had spent my life painting in oil as a hobby but I could no longer stand for long periods of time and was afraid the chemicals would do more harm to my lungs so I went looking for a new hobby. Strolling through the internet I found this book by Patti Medaris Culea on making art cloth dolls, the dolls were beautiful and I wanted to try my hand at it so I took some sewing classes and my first cloth doll was born. During the long process of making these dolls I realized that my mind was totally involved and focused on the project at hand and not my illness, so soon enough my healing journey began.

While looking for inspiration I found you could also make these beautiful art dolls using polymer clay so I purchased my first block of clay, found an online class by Deb Wood and sculpted my first mermaid. Deb is a wonderful teacher. I realized I had fallen in love with this medium so I took more classes and sculpted more dolls.

One day while shopping for supplies at artdolls.com I found that you could purchase a critique by master artist Jack Johnston. I was thrilled when I received my grades and an email from Jack inviting me to join the Professional Doll Makers Art Guild. He referred my name to Cherie Fretto, another wonderful master artist who managed the Guild. She took me under her wings and became my mentor in this new Apprentice Program that was being established. I would sculpt, take pictures and send to Cherie who would correct and inspire me through each step of the doll making process. I remember the doll I was working on got this huge crack on the leg and I was ready to give up and throw it out but with Cherie's encouragement and patience she became my "Ballerina" and won the 2015 Gold Contest Apprentice Award. That is when Cherie invited me to join some of the artist members at the IDTS show in Asheville.

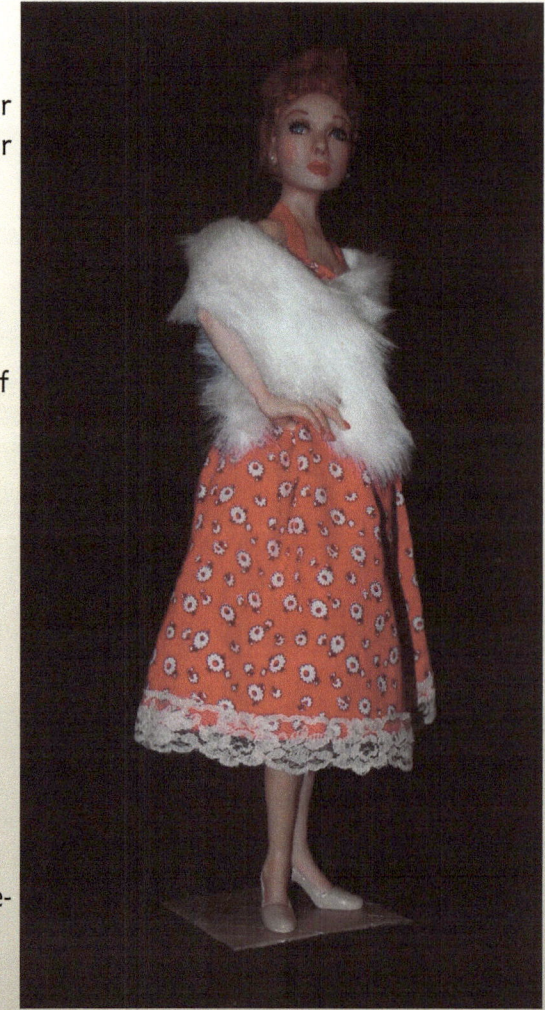

My Journey as a Doll Artist

By Esther Manso... continued

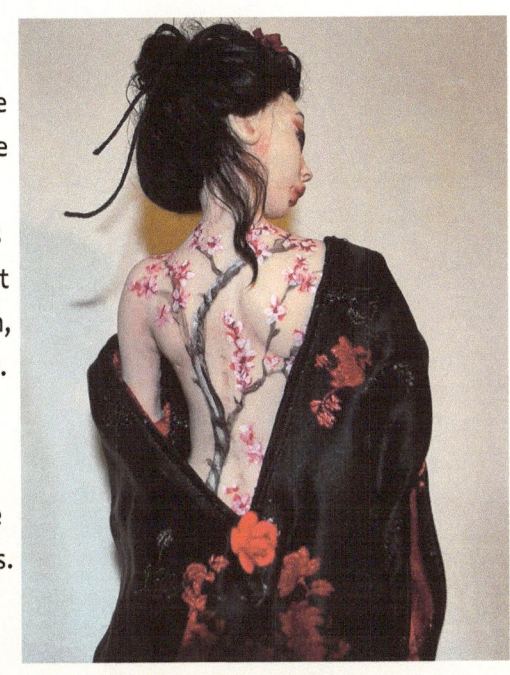

At first, I declined as I was very limited in my mobility and was very self-conscious and withdrawn but she made accommodations for me so I could be in the booth with my scooter and assured me she would be there for me every step of the way. Other Officers attended the show and some showed me how to set up my table and showcase the three dolls I took and Jack showed me how to price them. I met so many wonderful artists and acquired so many friendships. It was there that I received my very first PDMAG Gold Award at the gala Saturday night and if that was not enough, I also went on to win the IDTS People's Choice Award Beginners Category.

That was the beginning of my career as an art doll artist. I have attended more shows and my dolls have gone on to win many prestigious awards including PDMAG Gold Awards Advanced, Dolls Magazine Industry Choice Award of Excellence for 2016 and 2017 and many other Art Doll Challenges. Thanks to Cherie's encouragements and help, they have also been published In Pretty Toys Magazine. I could not believe that after thinking all was lost in my life, I was blessed with such wonderful people to help me find my way again. My plan is to go on learning and become a Master Artist and someday be able to mentor some new and beginning artists in this field so that this form of art can continue through generations to come. For the moment, I volunteer for the Guild and help in any way I can so I can give back some of the same blessings I received throughout my journey.

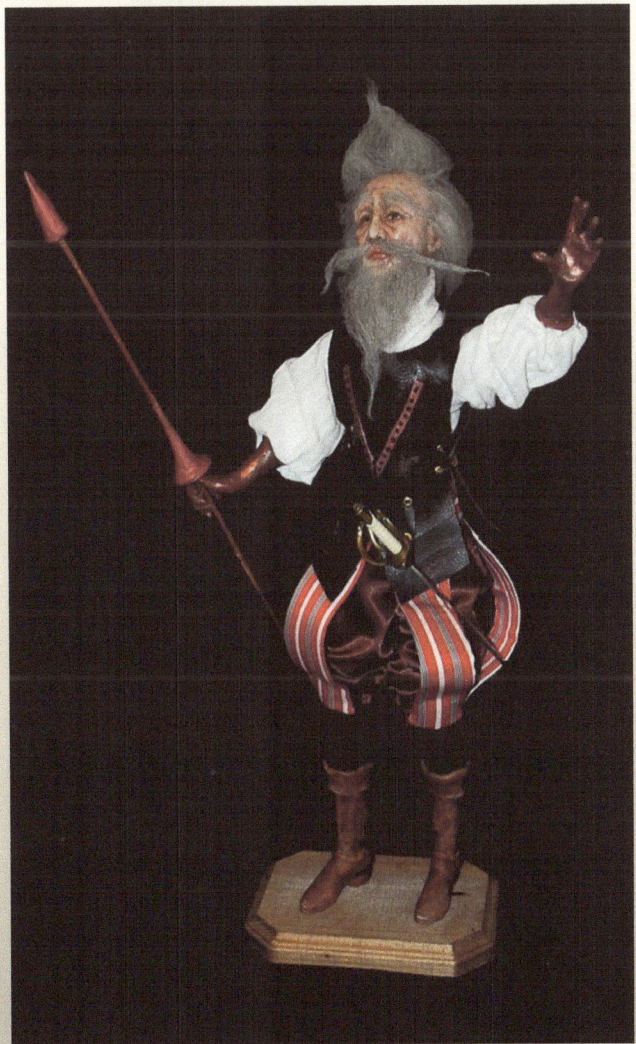

Today, the PDMAG has a wonderful Academy where new artists can flourish through a wonderful mentoring program either on a one to one basis or through our Facebook Groups. They are taught not only how to sculpt but are also guided on how to market their dolls and sell them. Many new artists have graduated since then, I am glad and honored to have been the very first one.

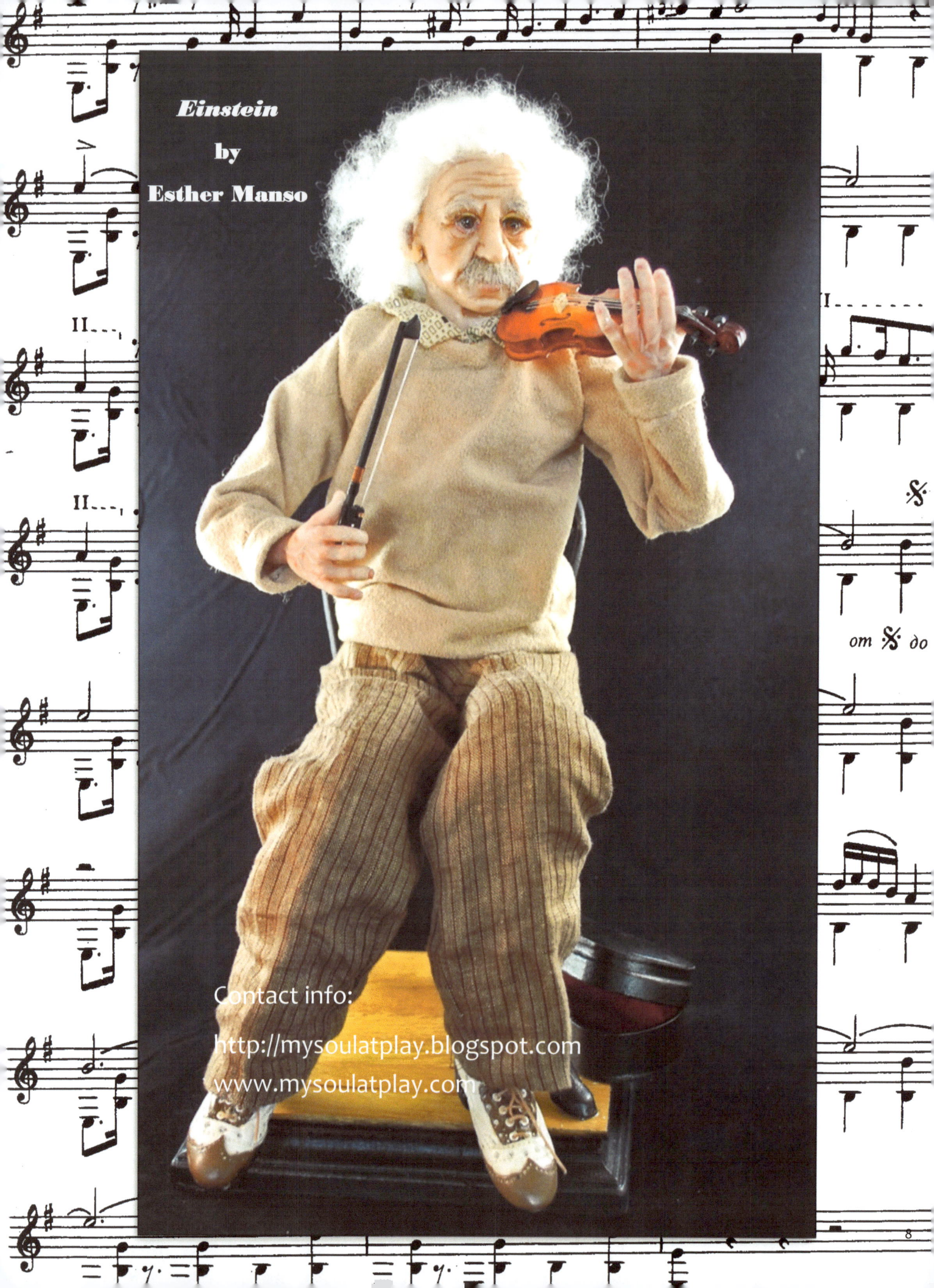

My World
by Alessandra Nicolin

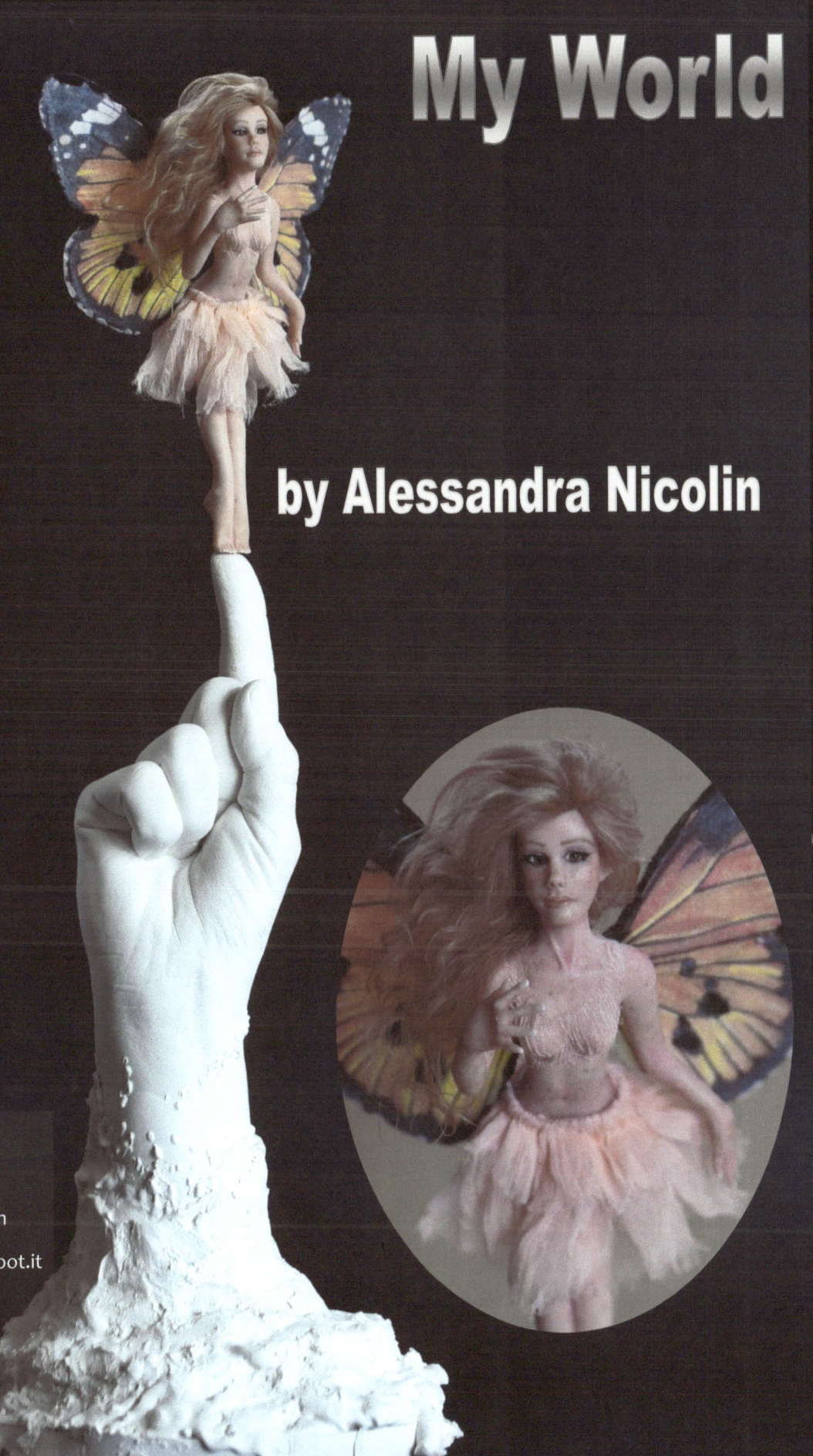

With the reproduction of her hand, she wanted to represent her world; so this creation can be considered her self-portrait, her true nature. Each of us sees the truth she wants, and truth can make her crazy....And you? Do you believe in fairies?

The whole creation is about 18.30 inches high. The fairy is 6.3 inches and the hand is 12.60 inches. The hand is plaster and is exactly the reproduction of her hand with alginate. You can see the pores, veins and even the small scars of her hand. It is fantastic.

The fairy is made in polymer clay and painted with genesis colors. The dress is silk and is glued. The wings were printed by her on cotton fabric to have a more realistic effect.

Contact info:

Alessandra.nicolin@gmail.com

http://alessandranicolin.blogspot.it

http://www.facebook.com/Alessandra-nicolin

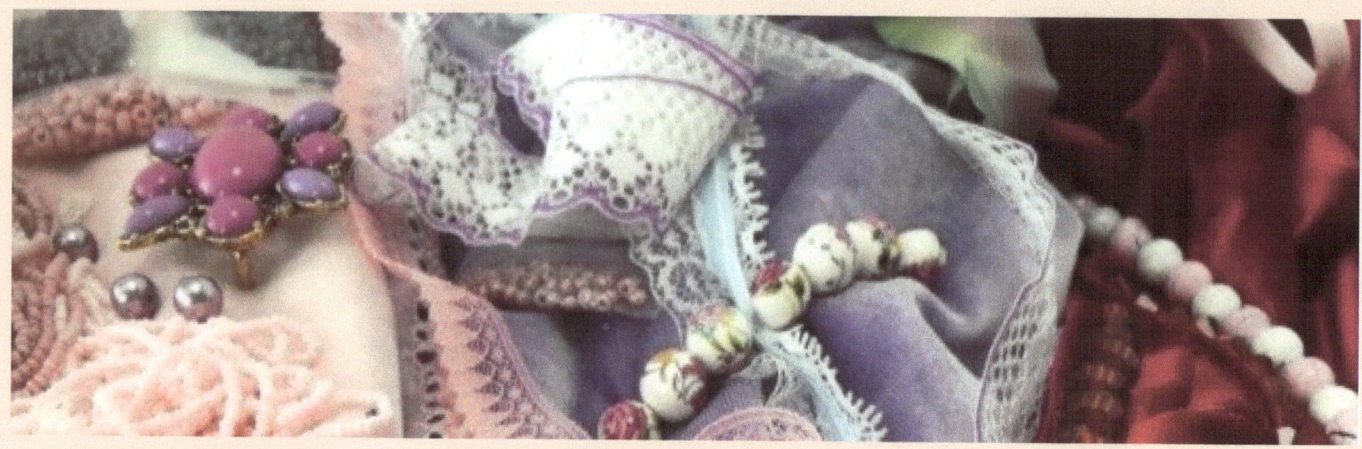

My " 50% by 50%" Color Rule

All of us like the Beauty of Harmony.....

By Marina Bondarenko

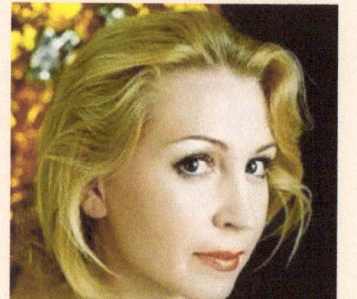

Article Highlights

Beauty of harmony

Famous Painting as your reference

50% by 50% Color Rule

Practice to combine colors

Listen to Yourself

Color Song

Have you ever asked yourself, while you were looking at someone's creation : How did she/he come up with this idea for the doll's costume? Why did she choose this particular fabric/lace/beads/etc.....? And then: -Hmm, I would probably have never even looked at this fabric in the store if I had had this doll idea on my mind...... Well, let me tell you, you are not alone. I do ask these questions myself as well. Yes, you, as an artist, have the freedom to choose any fabric combination, and if someone tells you it is kind of a strange or awkward choice, you can place it just in the right place and you really like your creation. Always say– well it is my creation, I can do whatever I want. But, let's be honest. All of us like the beauty of harmony and all of us are trying our best to reach that point of satisfaction when every piece of our doll costume is placed just in the right place and you really like every bit of your creation. I'm a professional seamstress and being perfectionist, I think, is one of my strength. It helps me not only make good quality clothes, but also push me farther to pursue the goal of creating costumes for my dolls, which are not ordinary. I like the feeling of satisfaction when I do it this way.

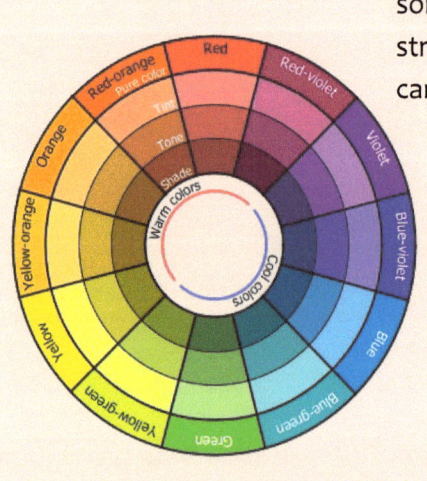

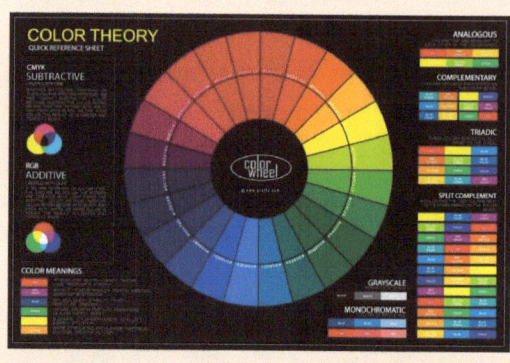

Artist Color Wheel

Fabric patterns - My Great Inspirations....

There are many strategies how to achieve great color combination in doll's costume. Today you can find many tutorials online how to use, for example, artist Color Wheel . It is a very great tool to learn how the colors work, while combined. How they accentuate and complement each other. In this article I want to talk about the color as well and what I, as a doll artist, taking into consideration while working on doll's costume.

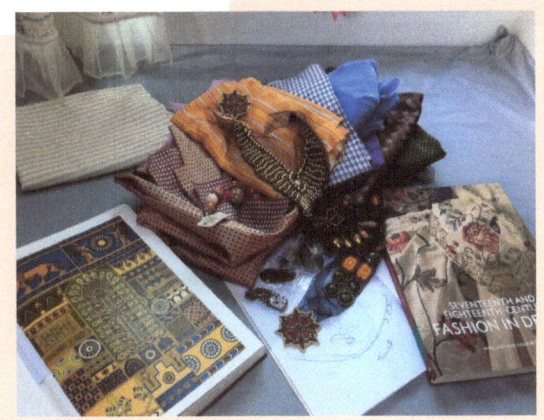

Useful Tools:
- Artist Color Wheel
- Try to Search "Color Cards" on Pinterest
- Great famous paintings
- Fabric patterns

You can use Famous Paintings as your reference...

Usually my doll's costume idea starts from the fabric. Even more, I would say the whole idea of a doll comes to me from the fabric. Interesting pattern or texture gives me an idea of what I would make out of it. It just strikes me and there is no way to ignore it....Listening to yourself is a good strategy while thinking about a color or texture combination as for a doll costume. When I begin to construct a doll costume, I like to use "50% by 50%" or "50% main fabric /50% balanced color for the rest" rule. What does it mean? Let's take a look at the picture (1). It is a great sample of how to develop a costume color structure . I called it a Costume Song. The main brown/orange fabric will take 50% of a costume and the rest I would divide in between. As you can see the last color in this row is light, silkish white with a little bit of blue shadow in it and I would definitely spend time looking for such a color, instead of putting a plain white silk, which is much easier to find. As for a dark gray/almost black color, we need it just a little bit, just to accentuate the whole picture. But I consider this color, as a very important accent, because on my opinion, without this accent, the entire picture would look plain and blended.

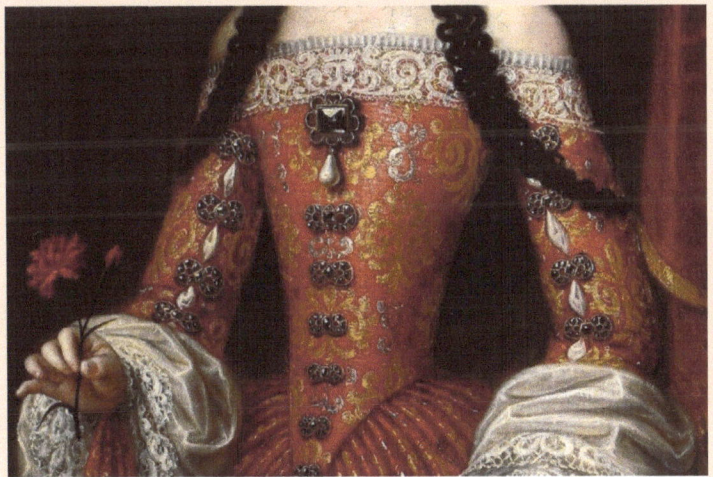
Picture (1)

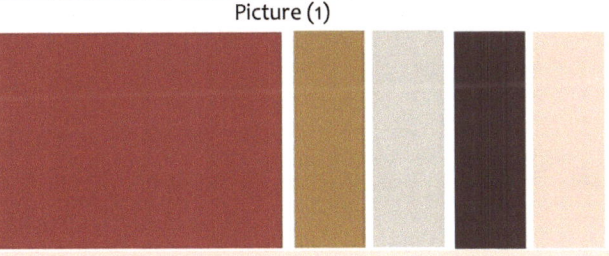

Regarding the texture – can you see how the sleeve cuffs are folded on the wrist, reflecting the light? If you keep looking at the sleeves, you will notice small openings along them, which stretch this light white/blue color up to the neck and ends this silky motif with the ruffle above a chest lace band. Same color, same texture, all over the top body. It is like a music piece with the right ending, with the right bit.

Main fabric will take 50% of entire costume...

Lets take a look at another great example. picture (2)

Black color is the main for me, so I would give 50% of my doll costume for this color. It is heavy, not stretchy velvet, for sure. Then deep cloudy blue- veil, sleeve cuffs, embroidery on velvet stretch this color over the entire dress, plus I would definitely use this color in beads combining it with two other blue-ish colors. A little bit of gold and accents in dark brown/ red.

picture (2)

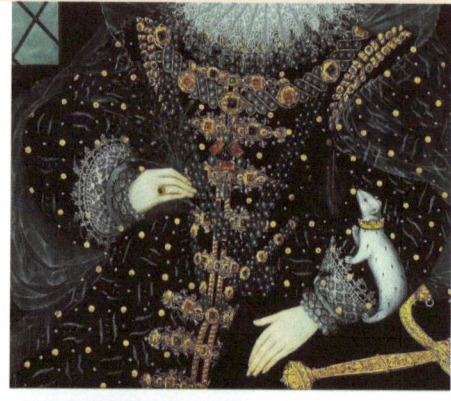

Now, picture (3)

Once again, 50% for the rich dark green (could be Taffeta, heavy silk or heavy organza), then olive suede, which creating a perfect pairing with vintage gold metal findings, then lace or silk, using two next colors and the last one is brick accent color. Well, it might be a good idea to use velvet as a main fabric as well. The velvet may not give you that strike shines that would give you taffeta or organza, but it would give you heaviness and nice folds on the skirt.

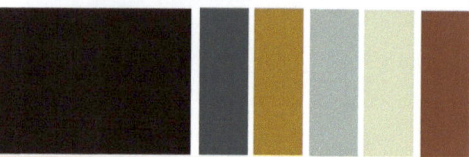

> There's no mystery to it. Nothing more complicated than learning lines and putting on a costume.
> Morgan Freeman

Picture (3)

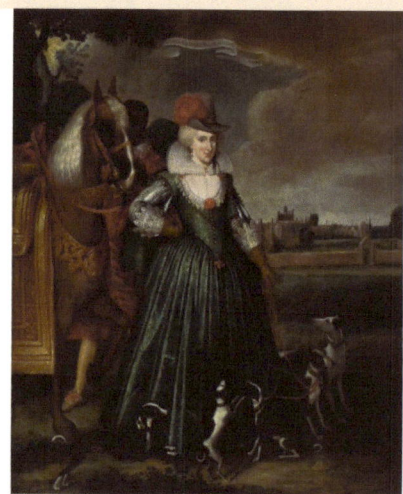

Portrait of Anne of Denmark, 1617, by Paul van Somer

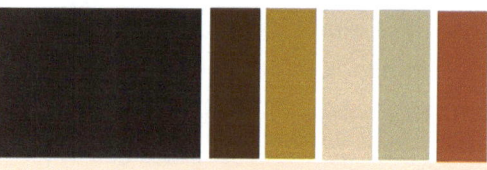

Practice to combine colors...

And now, here is my doll Annette. (4) Let's take a look at her costume. I used velvet in rich plum color as a main color. Then, two purple colors for her knee and neck fringe, then light gray for sleeve's lace which hanging all the way down. This color ties all pieces together, from the bottom to the top. Red & yellow colors for her corset and hat. Yellow gold color for accents.

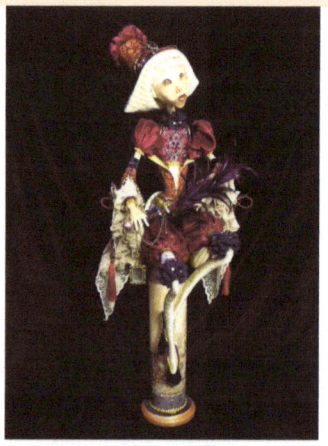

OOAK Doll Annette by Marina Bondarenko, 2016

It is very good to listen to yourself and ask questions. Do you really like the combinations? Do the colors speak to you? Do you feel the balance? Can you hear the Color Song? I was deliberating between two colors, light beige and deep violet, when I was thinking about feather stick she holds and it was my last piece that I decided to add in deep purple color as well.

> The thing that's great about being a costume designer is you never know what's going to be next; you never know what world you are going to enter.

| Main Fabric Velvet | Knee&neck fringe | Lace | Accents | |

Listen to yourself...and you hear the Color Song...

My Doll Sonette is on Picture (5). She has a monochromic costume and the very last color on the diagram is aqua blue. This color is an accent color along with antique gold. I didn't put it on the diagram, but there is the fifth color from the second part of my rule. It is goldish-silver which I used in metal beads. I really like white/gray stripped fabric in underskirt. Those stripes elongate her legs even more and helped me to balance her quite wide hair style.

As you can see, it is not difficult at all, once you start to think a little bit deeply and use good painting as a referral. Try to use this technique and you will see how your doll costume becomes more interesting, rich in color and in texture. And don't forget to listen to yourself– in most cases you are right.

Marina Bondarenko

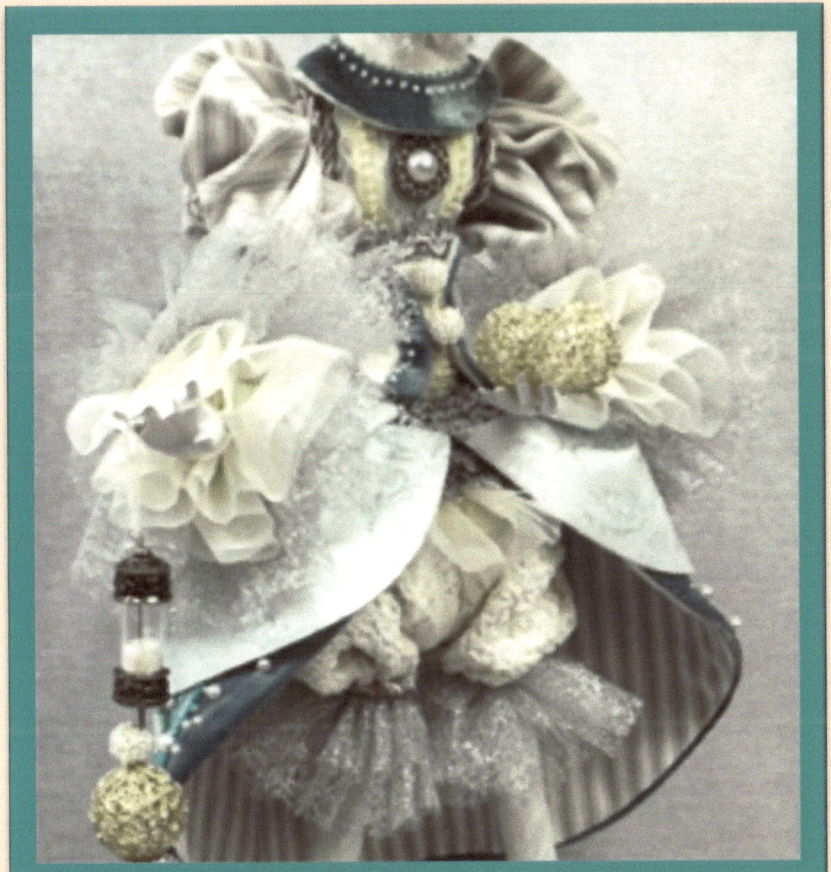

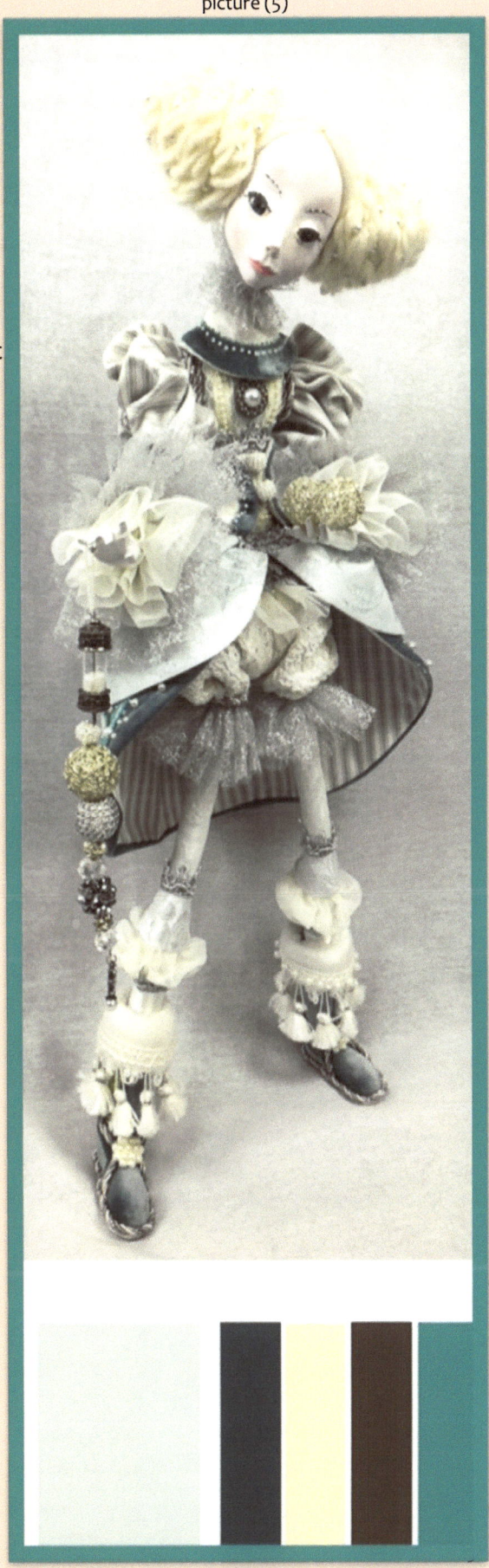

picture (5)

Marina Bondarenko is a professional seamstress, sewing teacher and a Doll Artist. Her FB page is : htttp://Facebook.com/MarinaBoudoirDolls, email: Maridolls777@gmail.com

Linda Lyons
Paper clay
Art Dolls

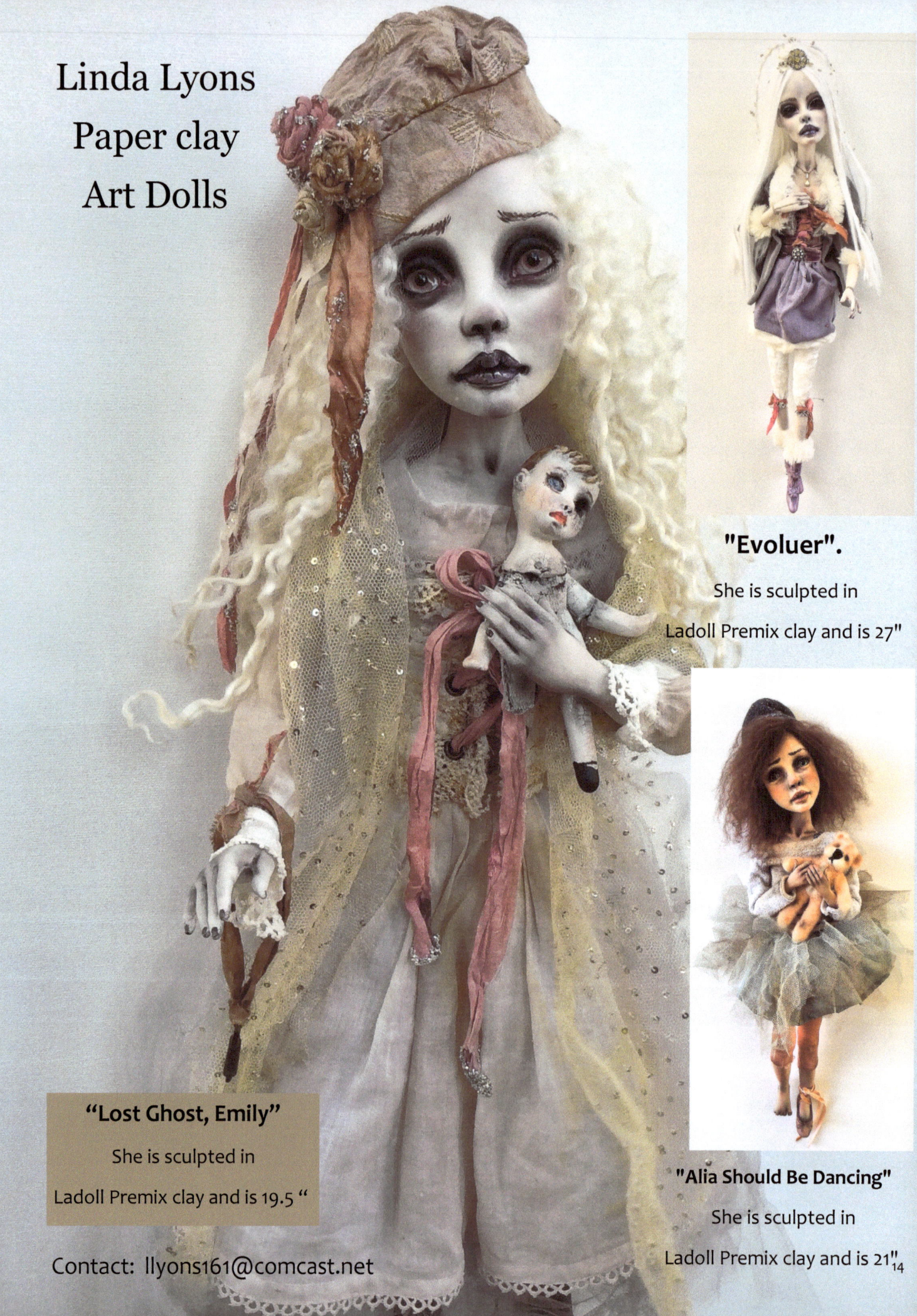

"Evoluer".

She is sculpted in

Ladoll Premix clay and is 27"

"Alia Should Be Dancing"

She is sculpted in

Ladoll Premix clay and is 21"

"Lost Ghost, Emily"

She is sculpted in

Ladoll Premix clay and is 19.5 "

Contact: llyons161@comcast.net

Beverly Warren

This doll was made for the fairytale challenge that the Professional Doll Makers Art Guild had during 2017. Beverly's doll stands about 14", displayed on a wooden plaque, designed with auburn mohair. Green painted eyes, brown hat with mauve trim matching her vest with a white cotton blouse with lace and pink ribbon trim, and white underskirt. The doll is a OOAK made from Prosculpt with two-toned brown shoes also made of Prosculpt.

Contact:

warrenblove@msn.com

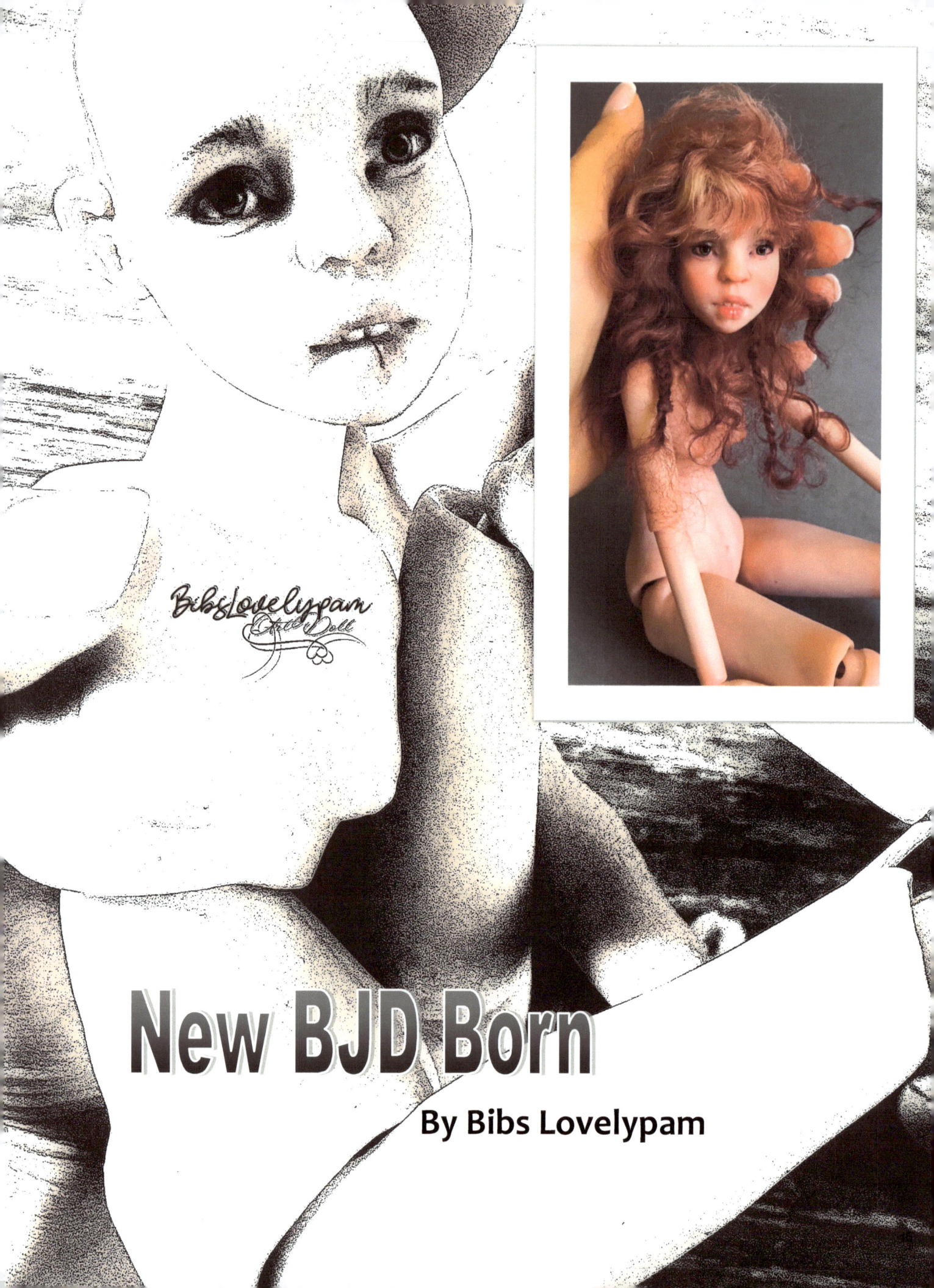

New BJD Born

By Bibs Lovelypam

Bibs Lovelypam creates her first BJD

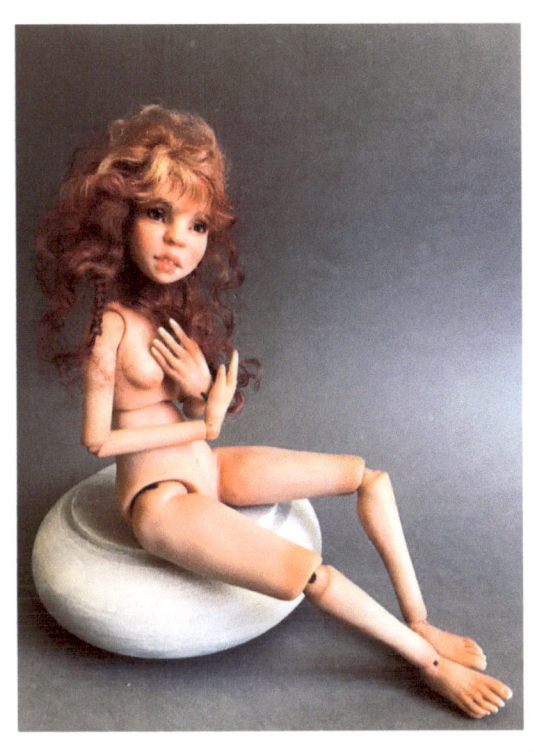

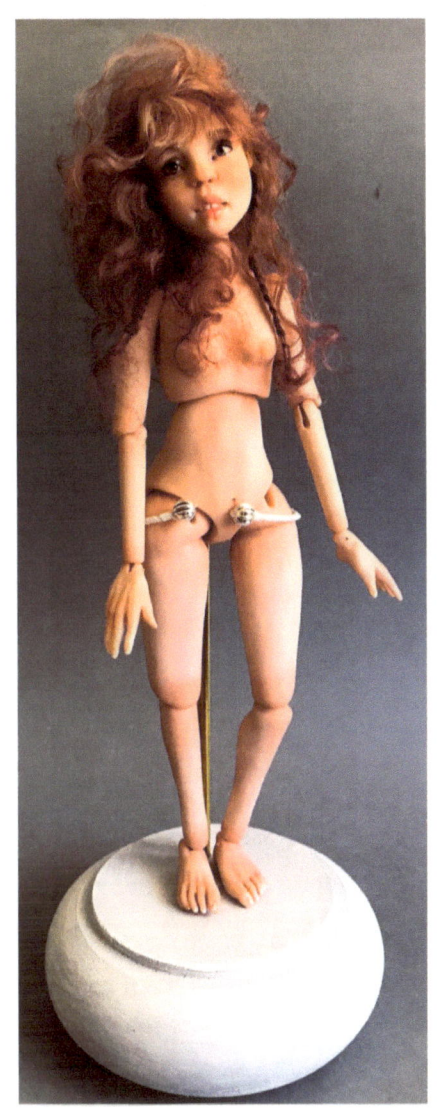

My experience with my first BJD has been so instructive !!! A lot of research on the internet, I watched a lot of BJD creators and I started. I used as a support a tutorial from Kori Leppart. But despite everything, I had to be patient. Many mistakes, which I corrected again and again. We only understand the operation when we start and we are faced with the problem :) At each stage I did not know how I would proceed for the next one. A fantastic experience, I learned a lot !!! I think next time I will do a lot better, some mistakes will not be redone. But in any case, I had a lot of fun, and I admit that I like it a lot. I think I conveyed by her emotion felt during its creation.

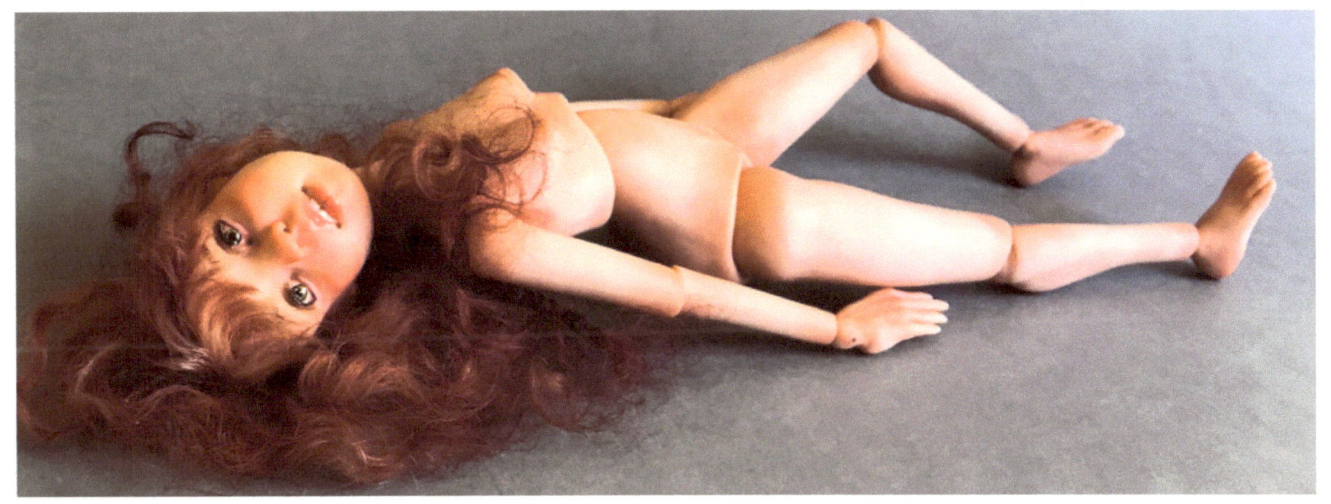

bibslovelypam@gmail.com

Illusion Costuming

By Kat Lees

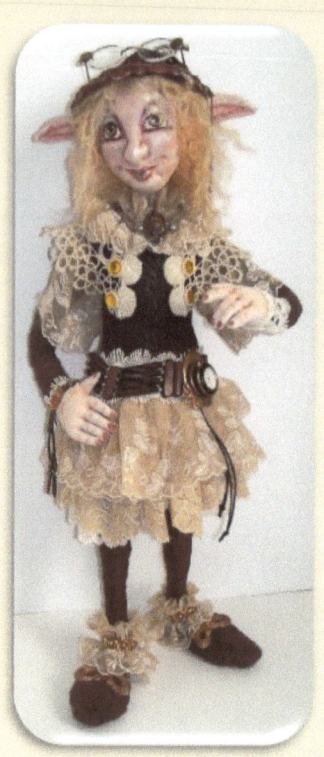

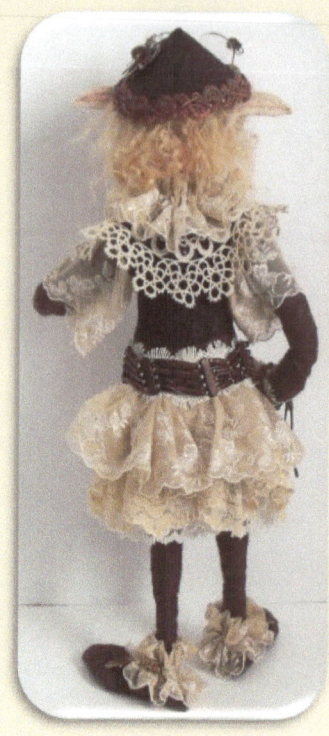

You ask, what is Illusion Costuming? This method of costuming is simply in fact creating a faux costume. This means it is not a completely finished garment as in one piece. You are making all of the parts of the garment to look as if they are a completely finished costume. They are all separate pieces added to the doll one at a time.

This type of costuming is not for dolls that are played with because the garments are permanent. For me it is a way to costume that goes faster and easier. I used to make my own clothing and did not enjoy the process at all.

Meet Gwyneth the Steampunk Elf

Simply stated "Illusion Costuming" is about creating all the parts of the garment separately. When you break down the components of the costume such as you see here on Gwyneth ~

I needed a skirt, shirt, sleeves, bloomers, shoes and embellishments.

The embellishments play an important role in hiding the raw edges, giving the costume a finished look as well as adding interest and detail to each costume.

I am going to use my doll pattern "Gwyneth the Steampunk Elf" as examples for this article.

You ask how do we create an Illusion Costume. All of the costumes parts are made from circles and assorted size tubes. For the skirt I measure the length first and then decide on the tubes width. The more you want the items to stand out

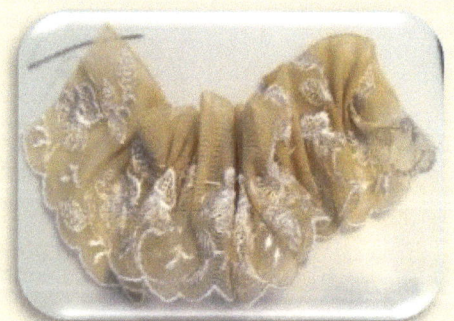
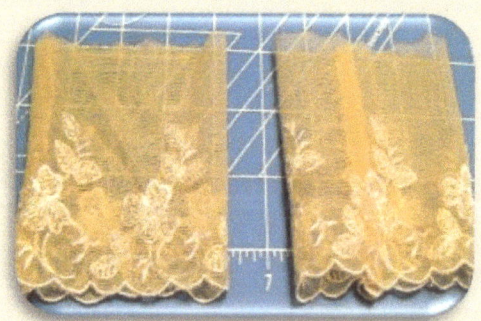
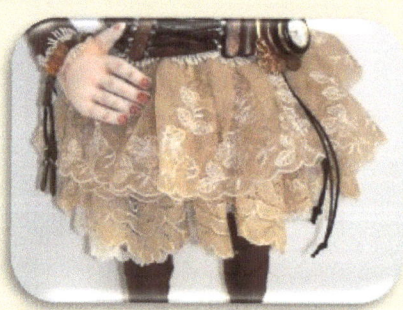

Above are examples of a neck embellishment, sleeve tubes and the three layers of skirt lace. The most important thing to remember when using this method of "Illusion Costuming" is it is all about layering each garment piece onto the doll separately.

Creating a great doll is all about detail whether you are creating a completed costume or Illusion. Pay particular attention to all the details, make the costume interesting. Study the photos above and look at all of the different items used to embellish this doll to bring her to life.

Be brave and step outside of your comfort zone, do something unexpected, make a statement with your work of art. What type of items do you see used on Gwyneth? Do you see a watch, necklaces, buckles, bracelets, earrings, tubes, ruffles, doilies, felt, trims, leather, laces, gears and gadgets.

Illusion Costuming by Kat Lees continued

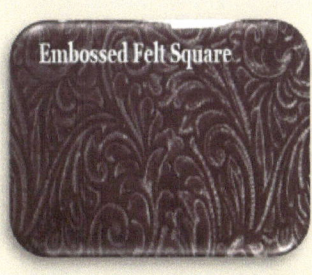

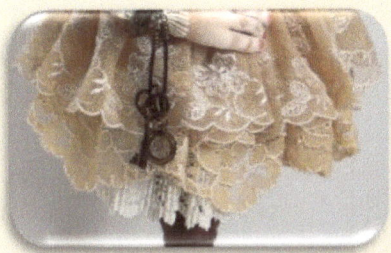

Gwyneth's body base is made of a wire armature and then completely wrapped in plain brown felt.

TORSO ~ I had this gorgeous embossed brown felt that I wrapped around her torso. I use hot glue or fabric glue on everything. I finished closing off the garment at the back of the doll using glue.

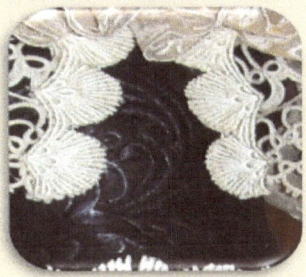

SKIRT ~ I used three layers of lace as you can see in the first photo below. Each layer will be a bit shorter than the last so I began with the longest layer first and worked my way upward. To achieve this I created three tubes from the lace fabrics by measuring each length and width needed for the Illusion. I wanted them to fall naturally over each other.

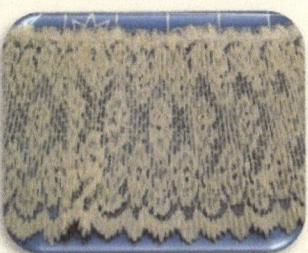
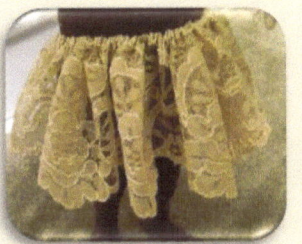

I ran gathering stitches at the waist areas of each skirt adding them to the doll starting with the longest skirt first. I smoothed out any bunches at each waist before gluing each skirt in place.

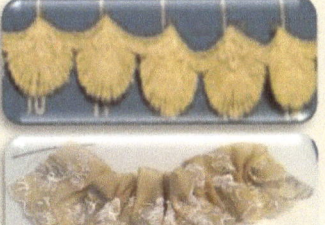
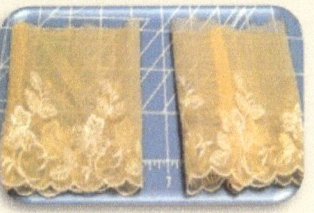

SLEEVES ~ I created two tubes to create the sleeves gathering them at the top. I then added them to the shoulders tightly pulling each in place. Next I cut out a design from a trim and added two rows as shown in the photo below.

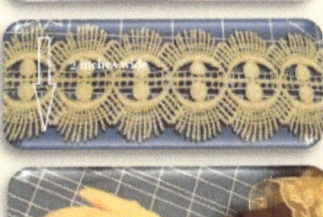
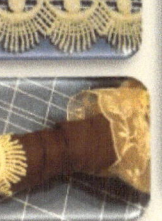
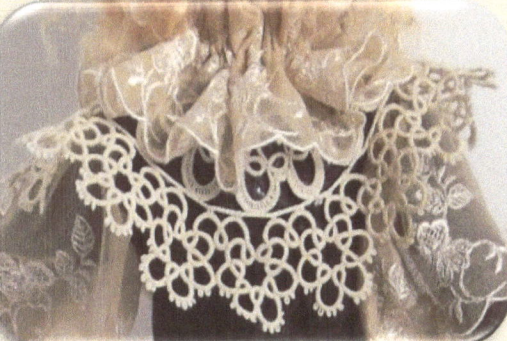
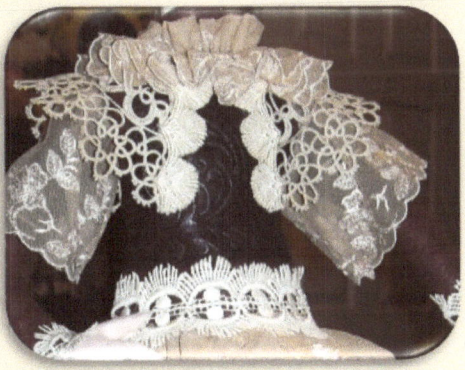

CAPE and NECK ~ to create the cape look I added a doily over the shoulders, cutting a hole in the center to fit around the neck area. Pin all in place until you see how it all fits together. Next I added the ruffle collar in place over the cape at the neck. The cape front will come just UNDER the cut out trim pieces on each side.

Remember all the garment pieces that have raw edges needed to be covered by another layer. All of the many layers gives the ILLUSION of a completely finished garment.

WAIST and WRIST ~ please study all of the photos. To cover the three layers of skirts on Gwyneth I added the full trim you see above to cover the gathered edges of each skirt. Do the same where the felt meets the wrist on the hand of the doll. I added the same trim.

Once you are happy with everything you have done then glue or sew all in place.

Illusion Costuming by Kat Lees continued

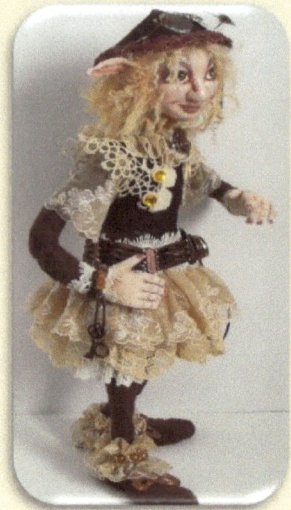
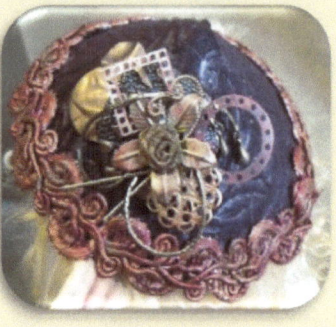
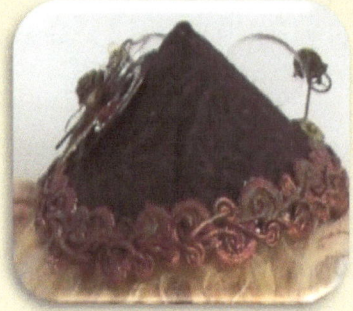
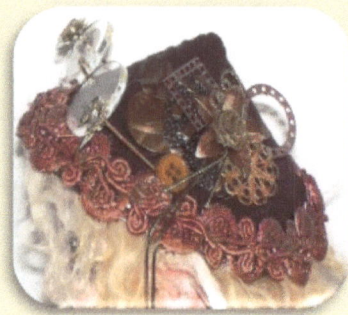

HAT ~ the hat base is made of the same embossed brown felt I used for her torso garment. I made a circle and cut a line to the center of the circle. I then brought the two sides together and glued shut (or sew). This created a cone shape for the Illusion I was going for here.

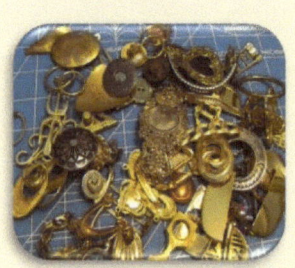
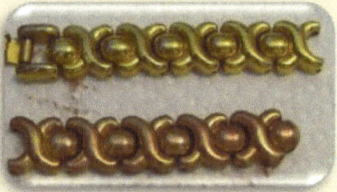
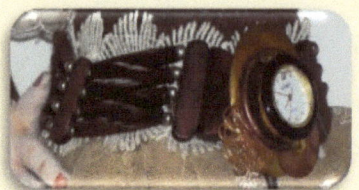
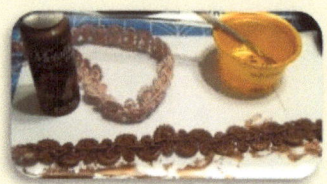

Next I embellished the hat with bits of jewelry and a variety of items. Study the photos here as I paint the embellishments that are not the right color. As you can see in the photos, the jewelry bits were a bright gold, and I painted all needed using a metallic copper paint.

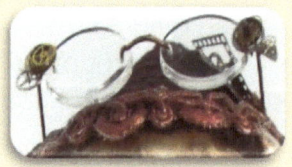

When all is decided I hot glued everything to the hat. I even embellished the eye glasses with a few gears.

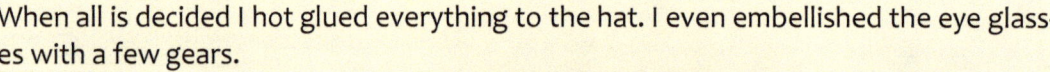
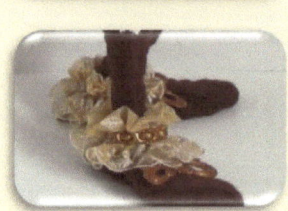
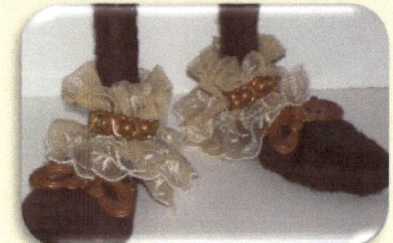
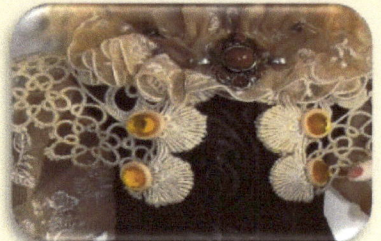
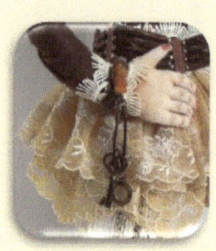

THE ILLUSION of SHOES ~ because the entire dolls wire armature is wrapped in brown felt the feet are already covered completely. I did not want to add an entire shoe but give the Illusion of a shoe. I save an assortment of bits and pieces of jewelry and unique items, so I have a great stash of embellishments. I began with making two ruffles gathered to add at the ankles. I then painted the bracelet the color needed and added them around the center of the ruffle. Lastly in the center front of what would look like a shoe I added an earring shape.

FINISHING THE DOLL ~ this is the most IMPORTANT part of your doll making, and that is DETAIL. It is imperative that you look back at the entire doll and see what may need more attention.
Above are examples of finishing the doll and accessorizing. The belt was added around the waist using a wooden necklace and watch end added for interest. It is all about layering. The shirt trim has faux gold buttons added, at her neck a necklace that was a bracelet. Finish the hands and finger nails as well. I added wrist jewelry for that finished look.

If you would like to make this doll go to ~ https://www.etsy.com/shop/designsbykat
Have fun stepping outside the box, try Illusion Costuming

~Fairy Spirit Dragon Art Doll OOAK "Shylee"~
by Michelle Albert

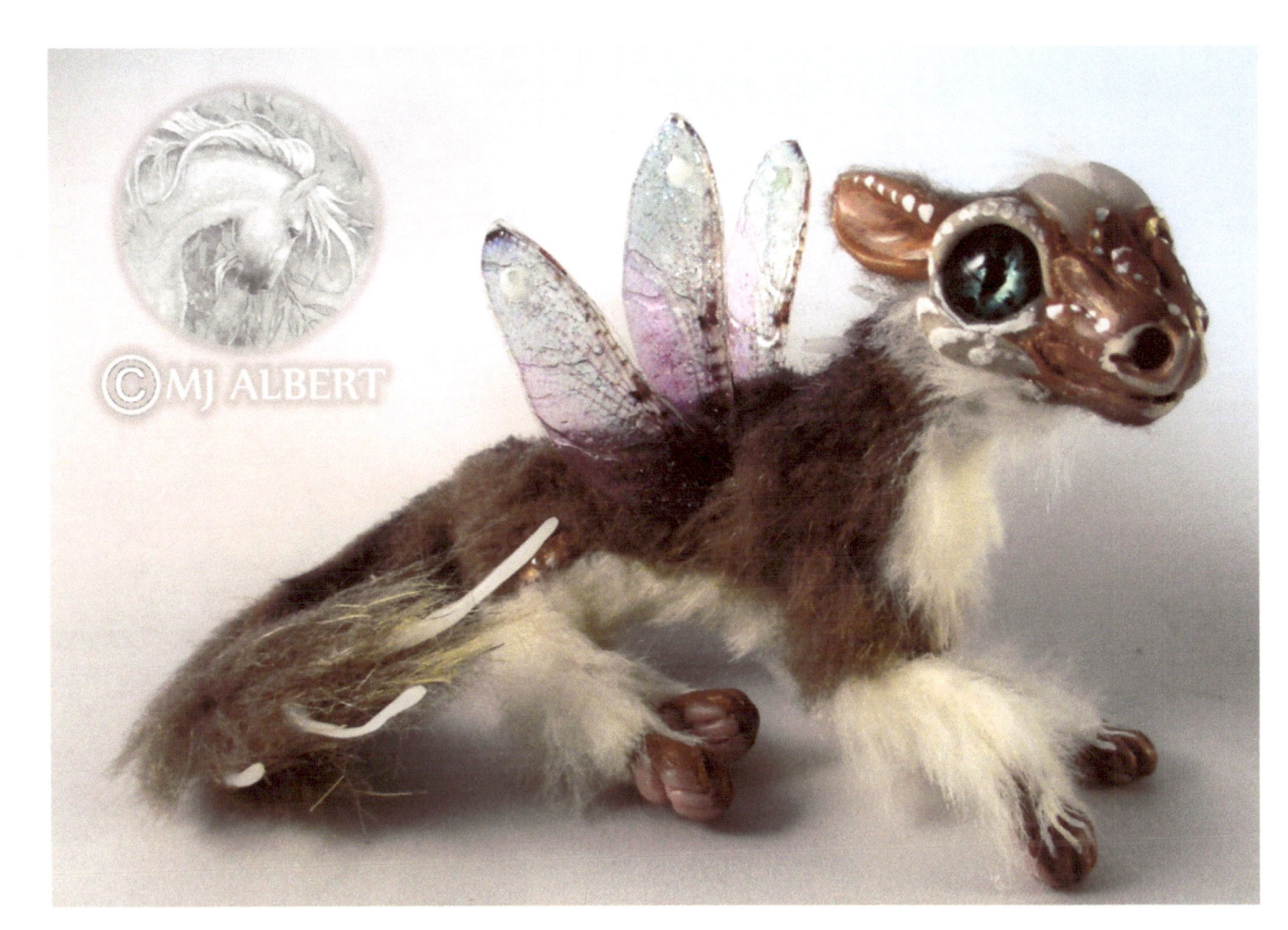

Fairy spirit dragons come from the land of fairy, and as such have the spiritual ability to enhance their environment and/or other creatures in our world. Although she is just a fledgling, she is already beginning to show her talent as "tranquility" which as she matures (fairy spirit dragons take a long time to reach adulthood), she will happily extend this essence to her closest companions.

"Shylee" is a one of a kind dragon art doll made out of polymer clay over a wire armature. Her size is 3" tall. She can be gently posed as you wish. Her eyes are handmade resin and her fur is a soft faux fur. No molds were used or cast. She's a true one of a kind never to be duplicated.

www.facebook.com/fantasyrealmartist
m-j-albert.deviantart.com

Costuming - A Creative Leap
A Journey for the Novice
by Marguerite Noschese

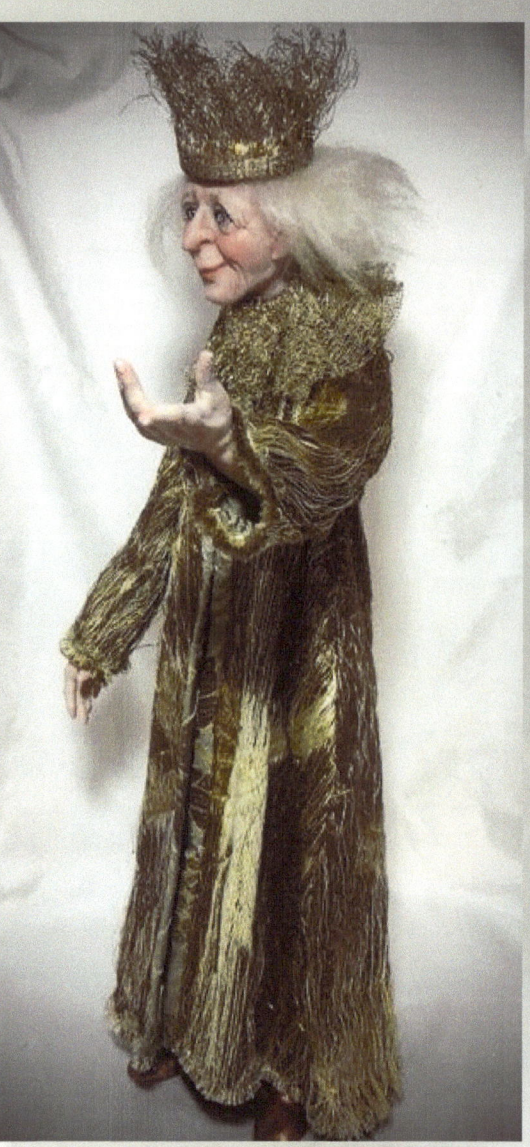

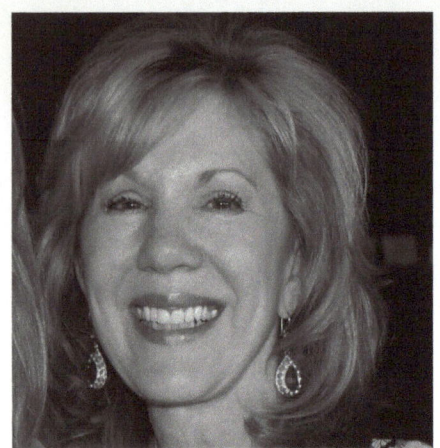

You have finished your doll! You have painted and wigged her and you are pleased with your results... and now you must dress her. If you are like me this is where the process can become a little more challenging. If your sculpt is an historical figure then there is clear direction on how to imagine your costume will look - for it will reflect the times and fashion of the period. However, if your sculpt is the result of your creative imagination then dressing the doll can be a little more daunting. What should she wear? What colors should I choose? How do I make a pattern? How do I begin! I have been in this position many times but have faith for it will get easier with each new sculpt. Most times I have a general idea of how I want my doll to look... a general idea of the mood I want her to convey. Then I sit and sit and stare and stare and proceed to pull every bit of fabric I own out and drape it over the doll. Yikes! There has to be an easier way. When starting the process of designing and dressing the doll one needs to start with an overall design concept. I must decide if she is a good/bad witch, a fairy, old or young, funny or serious. Most of us, when we start, are more concerned with the actual sculpting of the doll. Yet doll making is a multi faceted process that encompasses many talents. You may have never sewed before or made or cut a pattern. When I first started making dolls I had been a quilter and had a basic knowledge of my sewing machine and no experience with making clothes. I didn't know what kinds of fabrics to choose. I knew very little about techniques for aging or treating my fabrics. It took lots of trial and error before I found some generous artist friends (on the internet) who were willing to share their experiences with me.

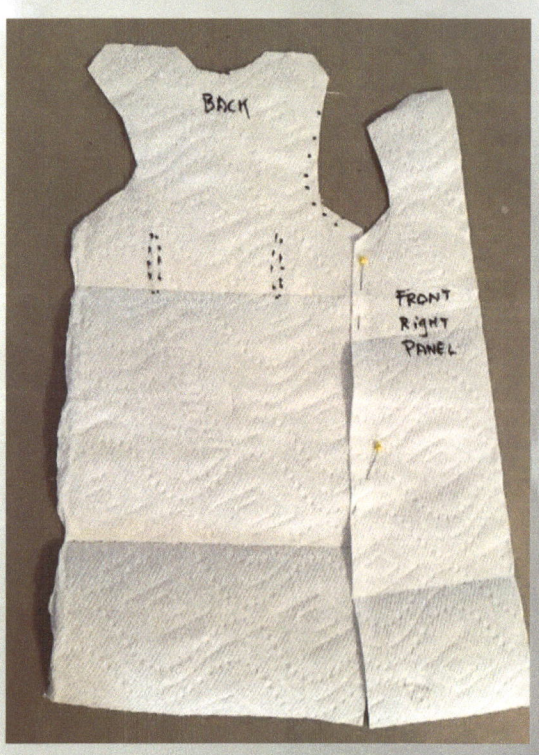

Costuming - by Marguerite Noschese - continued

A tip... don't add the lower arm of your doll until your sleeve is in place - if the sleeve is fitted. If it is a bell sleeve it won't matter. Also, do not over pad your upper arm - this will result in a bulky look to your sleeve....leave only a thin padding on the upper arm. I use the same general pattern shape for coats and jackets, long or short. I also like to line my coats/jackets with a thin material giving the garment a nice finished look. Although, if the garment material is thick I may skip this step. Always use natural material. Synthetic materials will not drape well on your figure and it will result in a very unnatural look. Avoid that at all costs! Also, wash your fabric if it is stiff..a soft cotton drapes well and adds to the overall design. Silks, cottons, linens, silk velvets are all wonderful material to work with. Vintage garments can be repurposed to create beautiful undergarments, slips and blouses. Keep an eagle eye on scale... a print that is too large for the sculpt will ruin a good design.

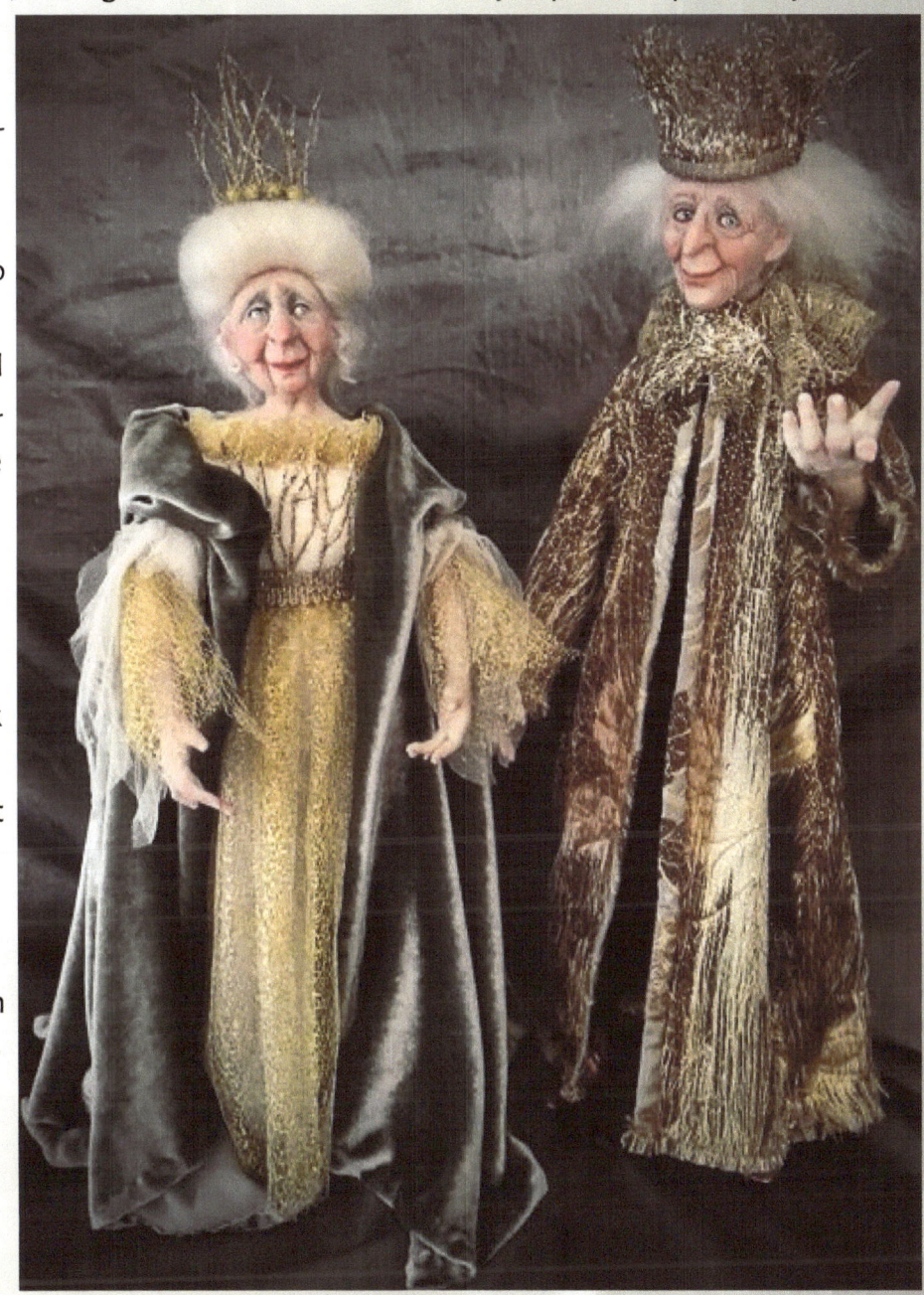

The first artist I asked (whose work I loved) how to start with the design and planning of a costume just laughed! She shared with me that she knew nothing about making dresses when she started and her whole plan was to just jump in with both feet and begin. Well, that didn't tell me much (I thought) but actually she was right. I began looking at some of my favorite artists work and studying how they dressed their dolls. While I had no training in making a dress, or jacket, or hat slowly I developed ways and techniques.

First I'd like to suggest to you that there are many wonderful books you can use to begin this journey. The ones that I have found most helpful are, well, anything by Susanna Oroyan: "Finishing the Figure", "Designing the Doll", or "Anatomy of a Doll". Also use Pinterest - there are many boards with great tutorials and information and creating costumes.

Costuming - by Marguerite Noschese - continued

Also helpful are Pictorial Archive books that have illustrations and fashion patterns from just about any time frame. Two that I have used are "60 Civil War-Era Fashion Patterns" by Kristina Seleshanko, and "Shoes, Hats and Fashion Accessories 1850-1940" by Carol Belanger Grafton. My technique when I begin the process of designing is to cut the pattern directly onto the figure. Since each doll is different there is not one pattern to fit each doll. I begin pattern making using paper towels! Yes, paper towels. They usually are long enough and strong enough that I can cut and tape the pieces together, if needed. After I decide on the general costume I want to make I will measure out each piece of paper on the doll. When making a coat, for instance, you will have two front panels and one or two back panels (depending on how you want the garment to fall). I will draw, measure, and cut each piece separately on the doll - I do this because depending on the pose of the doll the two front panels may be cut slightly different. Once the pieces are cut and pinned to the figure I make any needed adjustments . Then I will lay out the pattern on thin cotton material and cut (always allowing for at least 1/4 inch seam). I will sew the straight edges of the garment (either with a quick hand stitch or machine) and once again pin it to the figure. It is at this point that I will make additional adjustments and mark the garment if I need to make any darts for a better fit. Only when I am completely satisfied with the fit will I cut the material I have chosen for the final garment. Measure twice and cut once... or measure three or four times if you are me! I measure, cut, and place my sleeves before fitting my final coat or jacket, leaving a little additional fabric at the shoulder... I will tap that down with a quick stitch and then drape the coat over the fabric and sew into place. This gives a nice finished look to the coat.

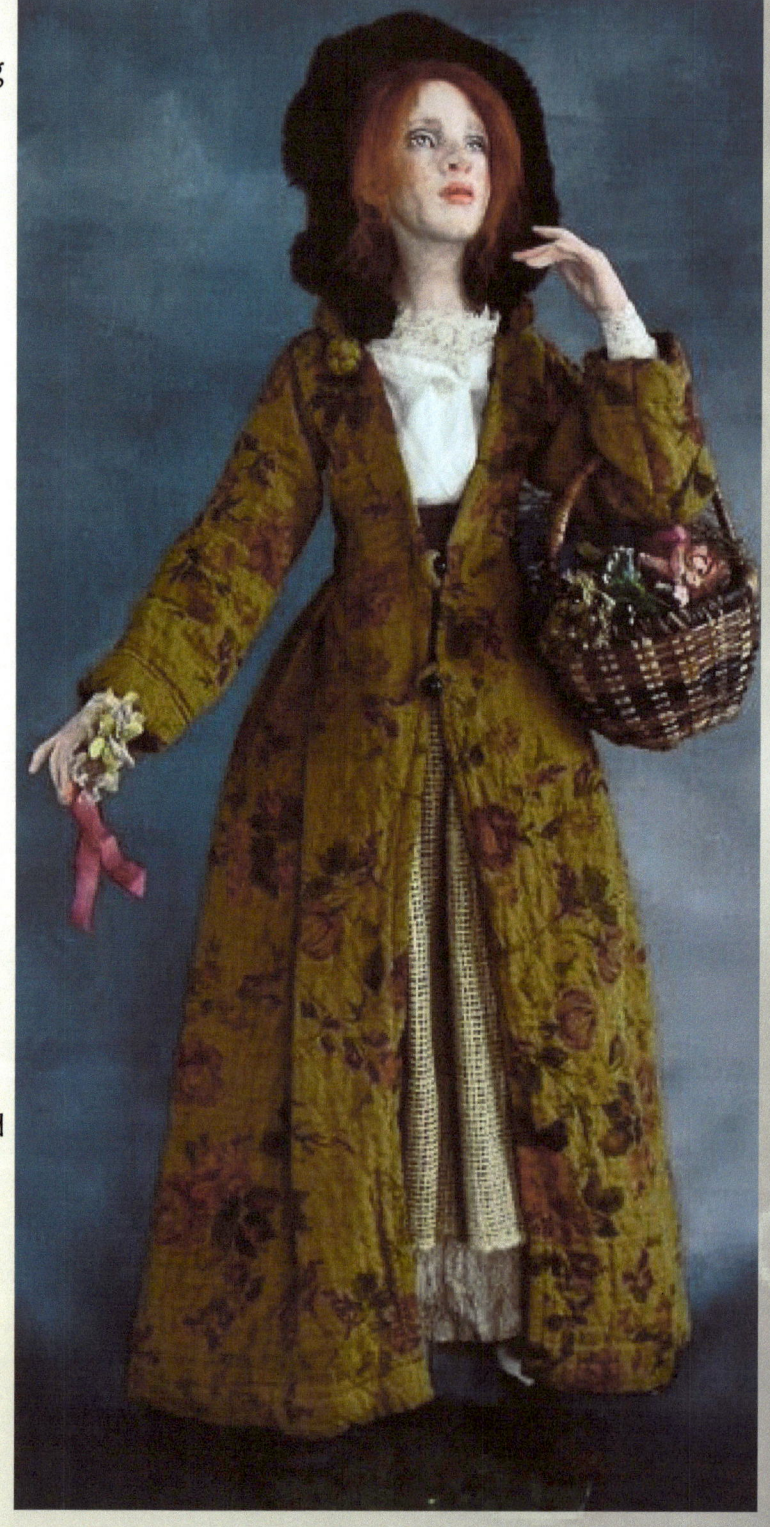

Marguerite-Noschese

Mywitcheywomen@me.com

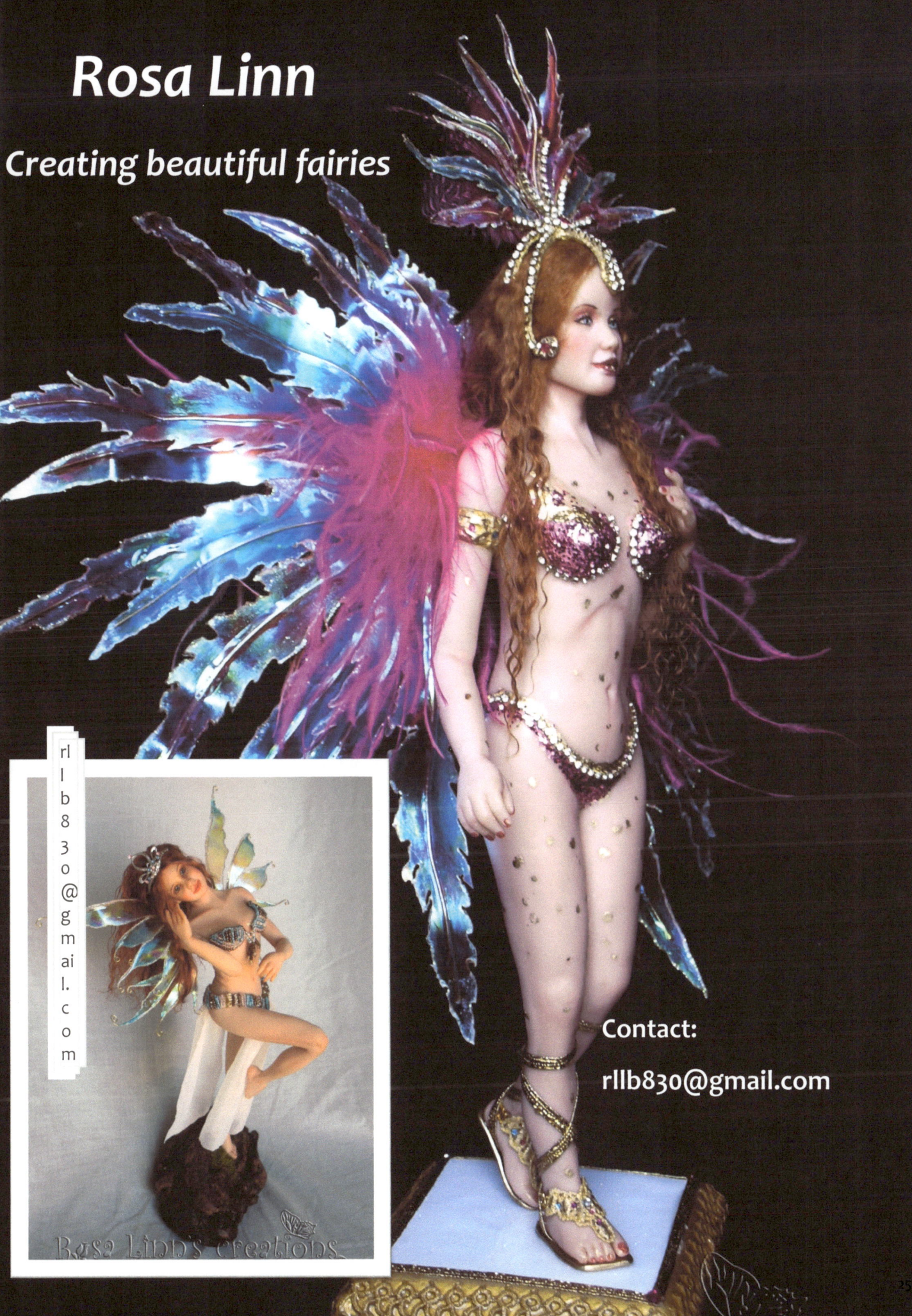

Rosa Linn

Creating beautiful fairies

Contact:

rllb830@gmail.com

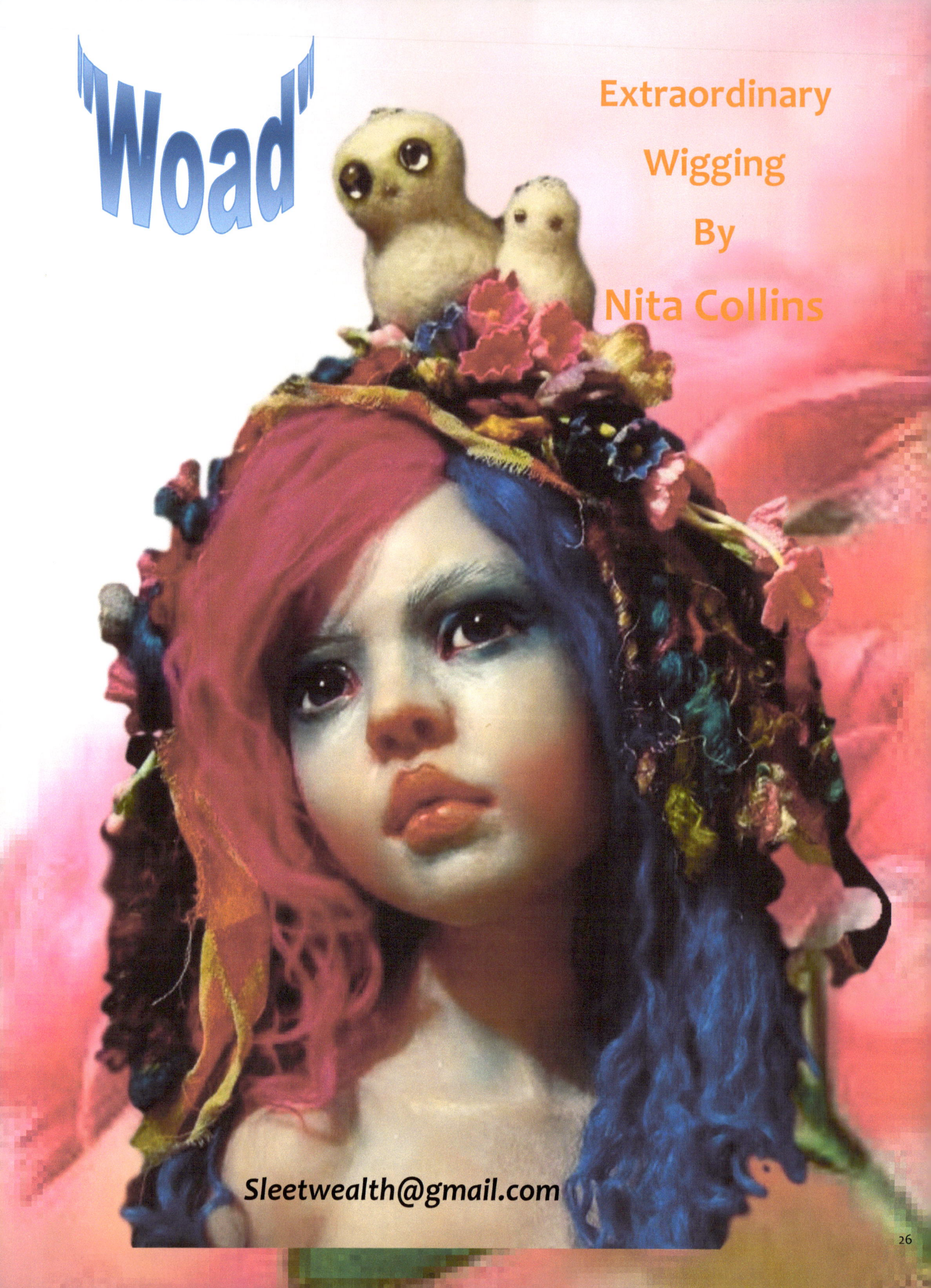

Laura Lafauci

lauralf73@virgilio.it

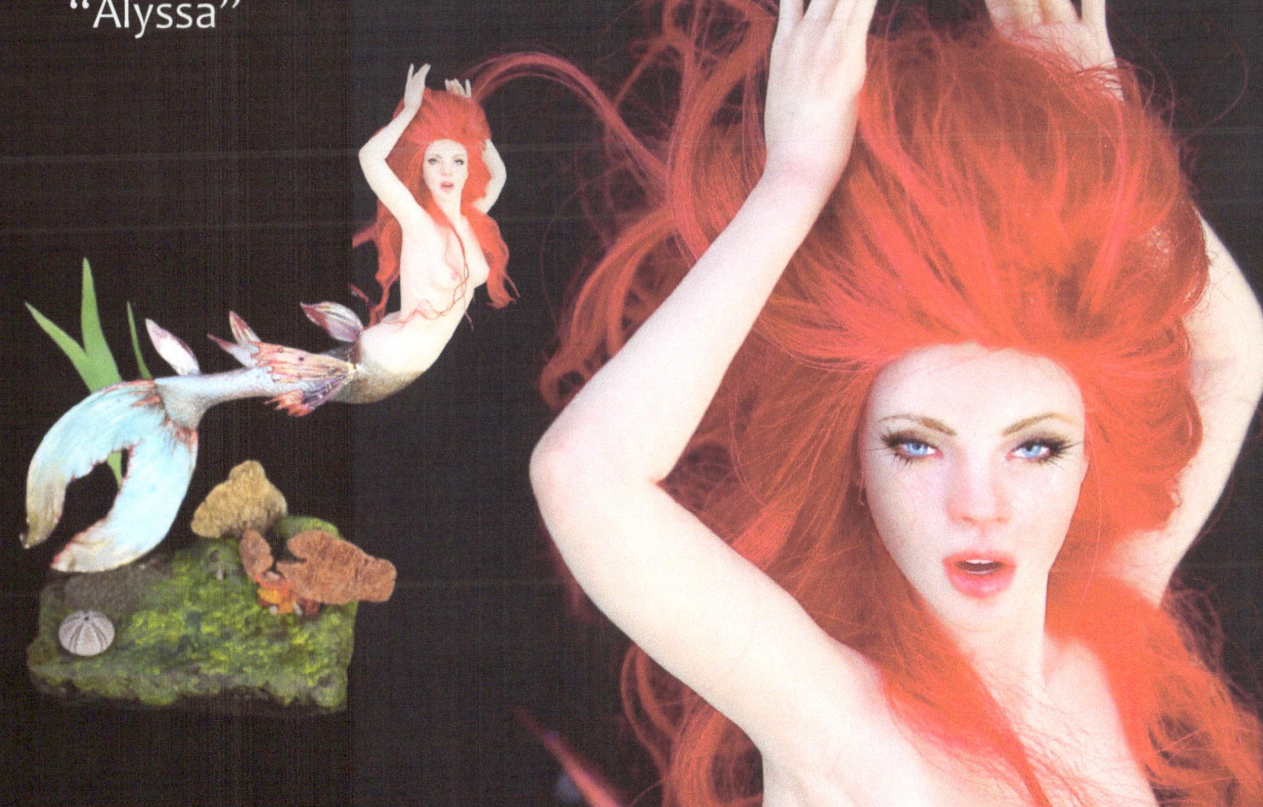

"Alyssa"

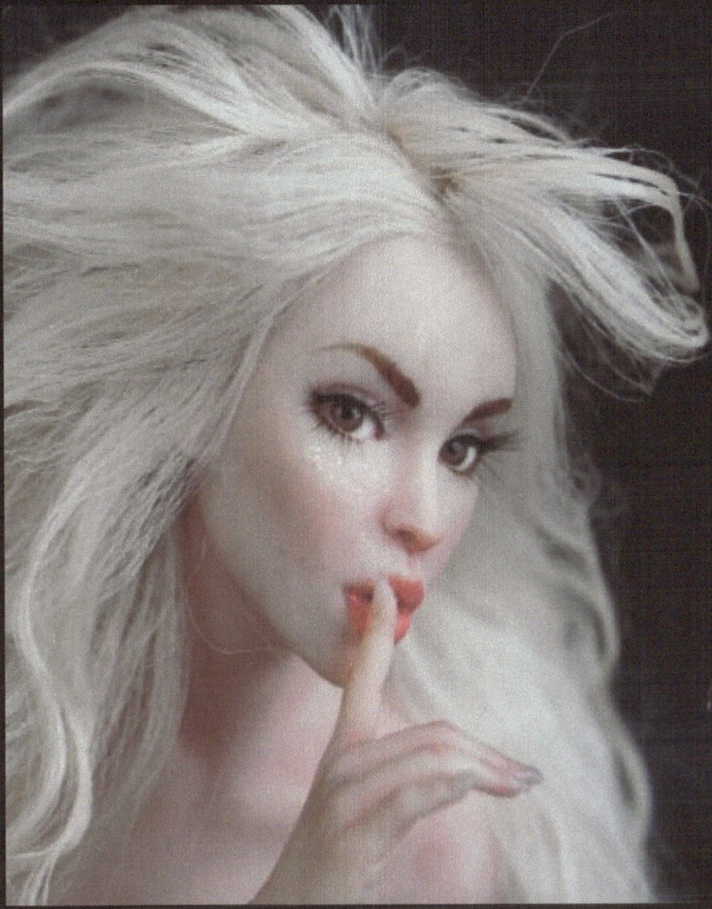

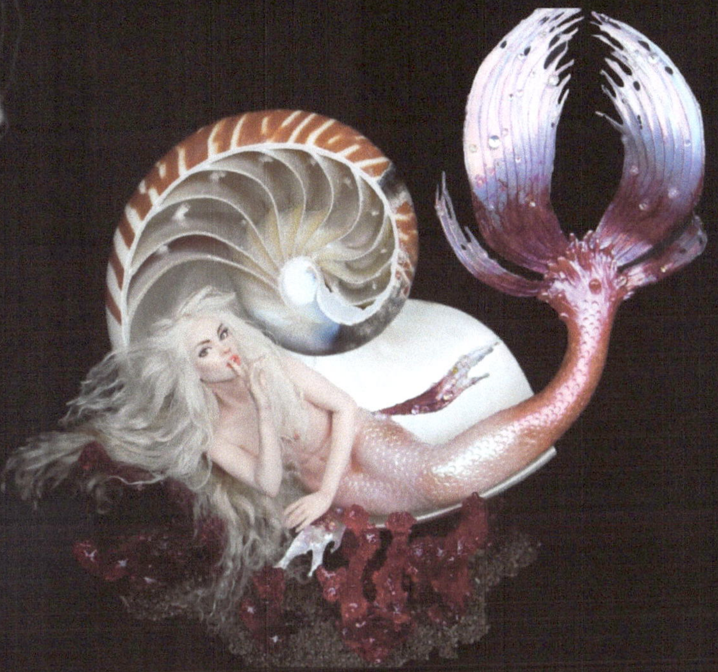

"Don't Tell Anyone"

http://ooakfantasyworld.weebly.com

Creating movement in fabric

By Vladlena (Jelena) Mihailova

lenalisa@inbox.lv

vladlenadoll.com

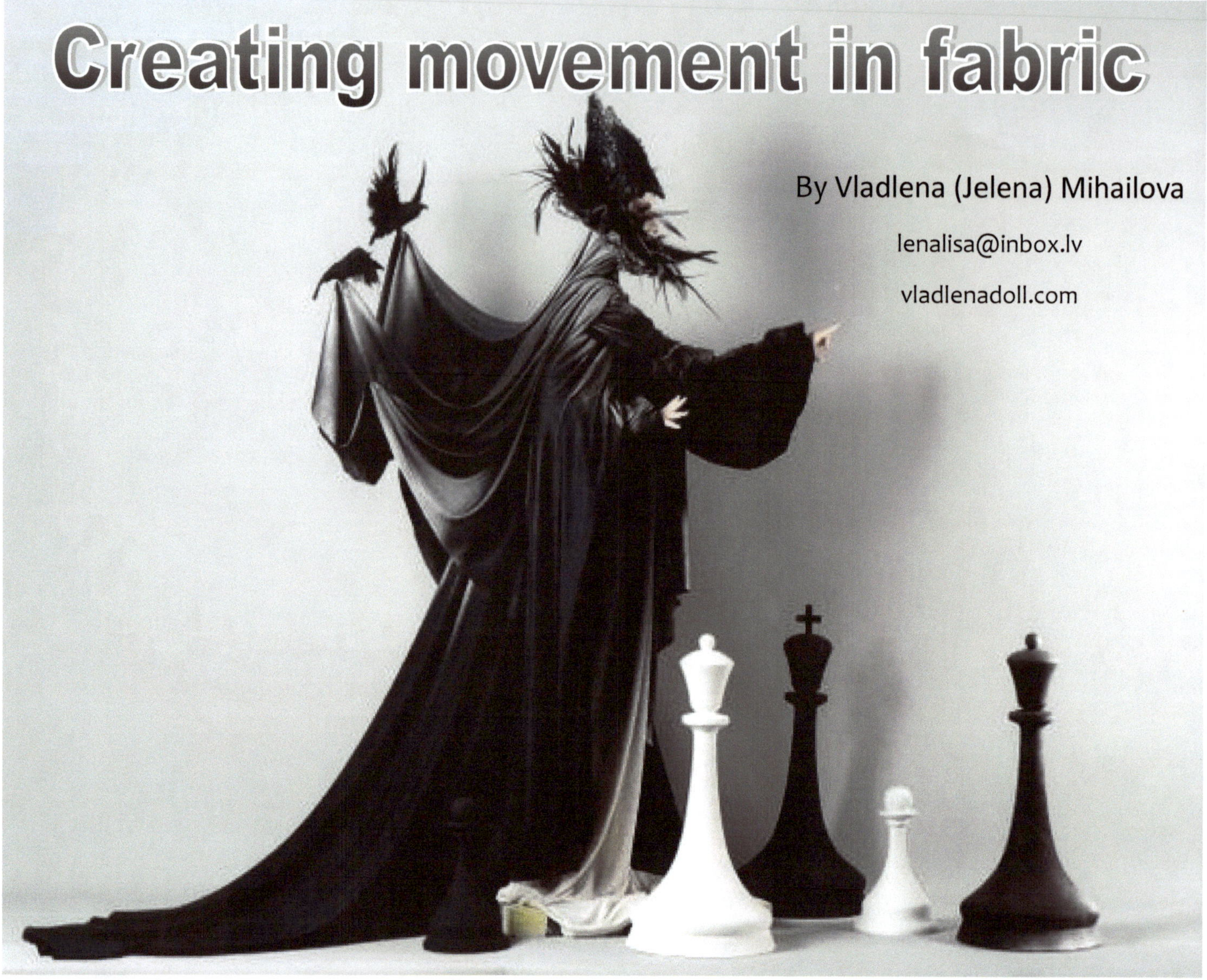

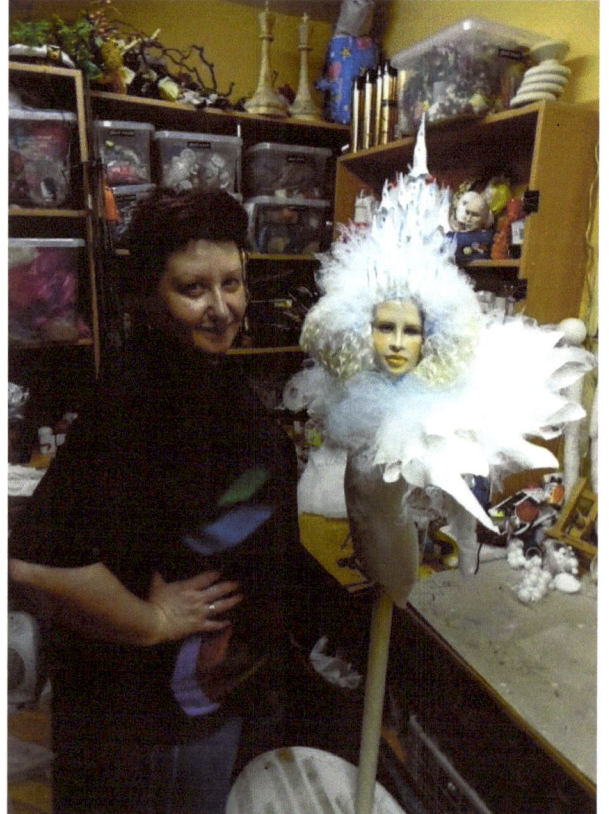

I think that the costume is one of the main parts of an Art doll and it requires a lot of time and effort. Before I start working with the fabrics I will use, I think about what it should be in ready form and how the finished piece will look. If it's a fabric that must fly or give the impression of movement then I prepare a whole wire frame that includes the armature and the sections to support the fabric. I attach it to the main costume with thick thread to allow for tension. Then I glue the fabric over the frame and for the hats. I use PVA glue and I use heavy fabrics on the frame so that I can not see the wire.

Creating movement in fabric Continued

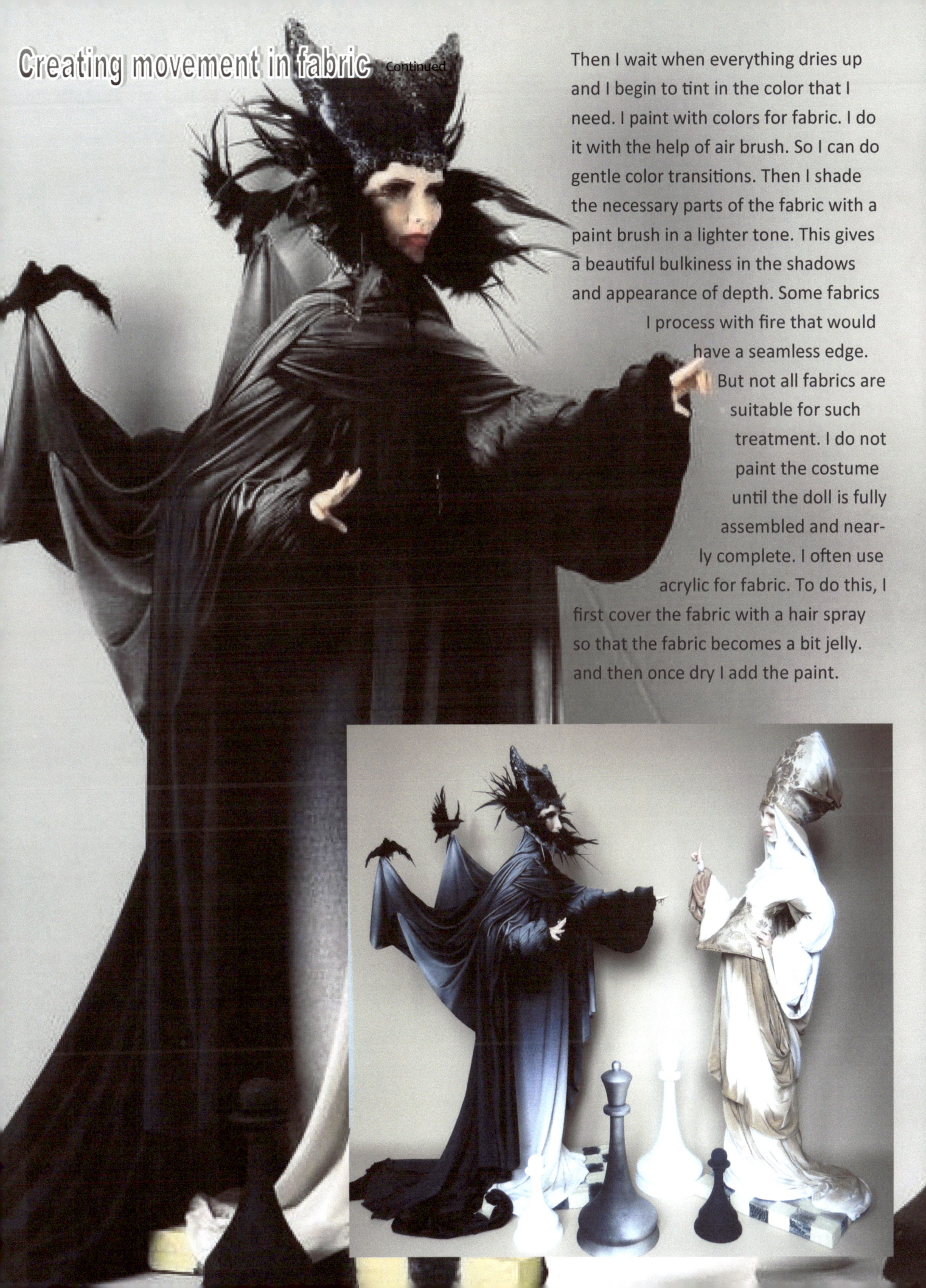

Then I wait when everything dries up and I begin to tint in the color that I need. I paint with colors for fabric. I do it with the help of air brush. So I can do gentle color transitions. Then I shade the necessary parts of the fabric with a paint brush in a lighter tone. This gives a beautiful bulkiness in the shadows and appearance of depth. Some fabrics I process with fire that would have a seamless edge. But not all fabrics are suitable for such treatment. I do not paint the costume until the doll is fully assembled and nearly complete. I often use acrylic for fabric. To do this, I first cover the fabric with a hair spray so that the fabric becomes a bit jelly. and then once dry I add the paint.

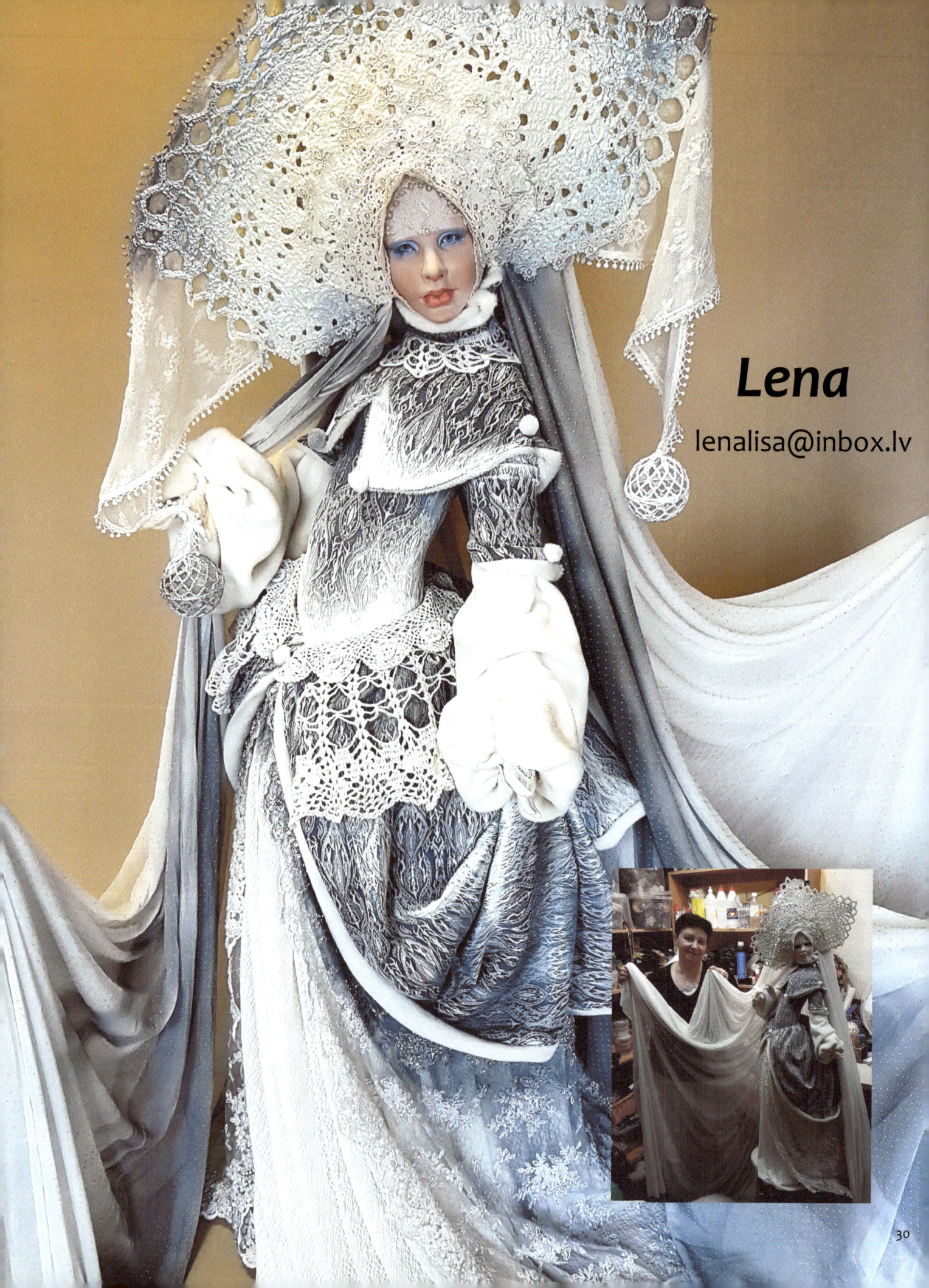

Lena

lenalisa@inbox.lv

Little Miss Scarecrow

Murielle Giannini

Little Miss Scarecrow is a poseable doll about 22cm tall, OOAK, completely handmade with polymer clay, genesis and acrylic paints, fabrics and tibetan hair.

mumughu@gmail.it

Facebook.com/Giannini.murielle

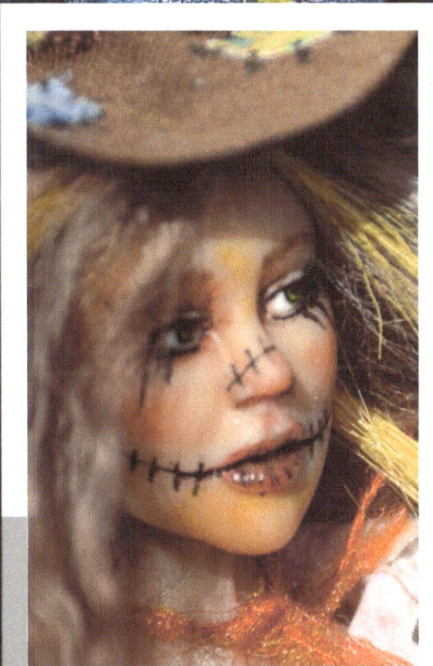

Endora the Witch

Endora is made from prosculpt polymer clay over a wire armature. Her feet have tubes in them for a doll stand. Her hair is made from Cotswold wool and her clothes are cotton. She is painted with genesis paints. Made by Alicia Sandlin at Miserable Moppets, ready for her showcase

Alicia Wilkinson

https://www.facebook.com/miserablemoppets/

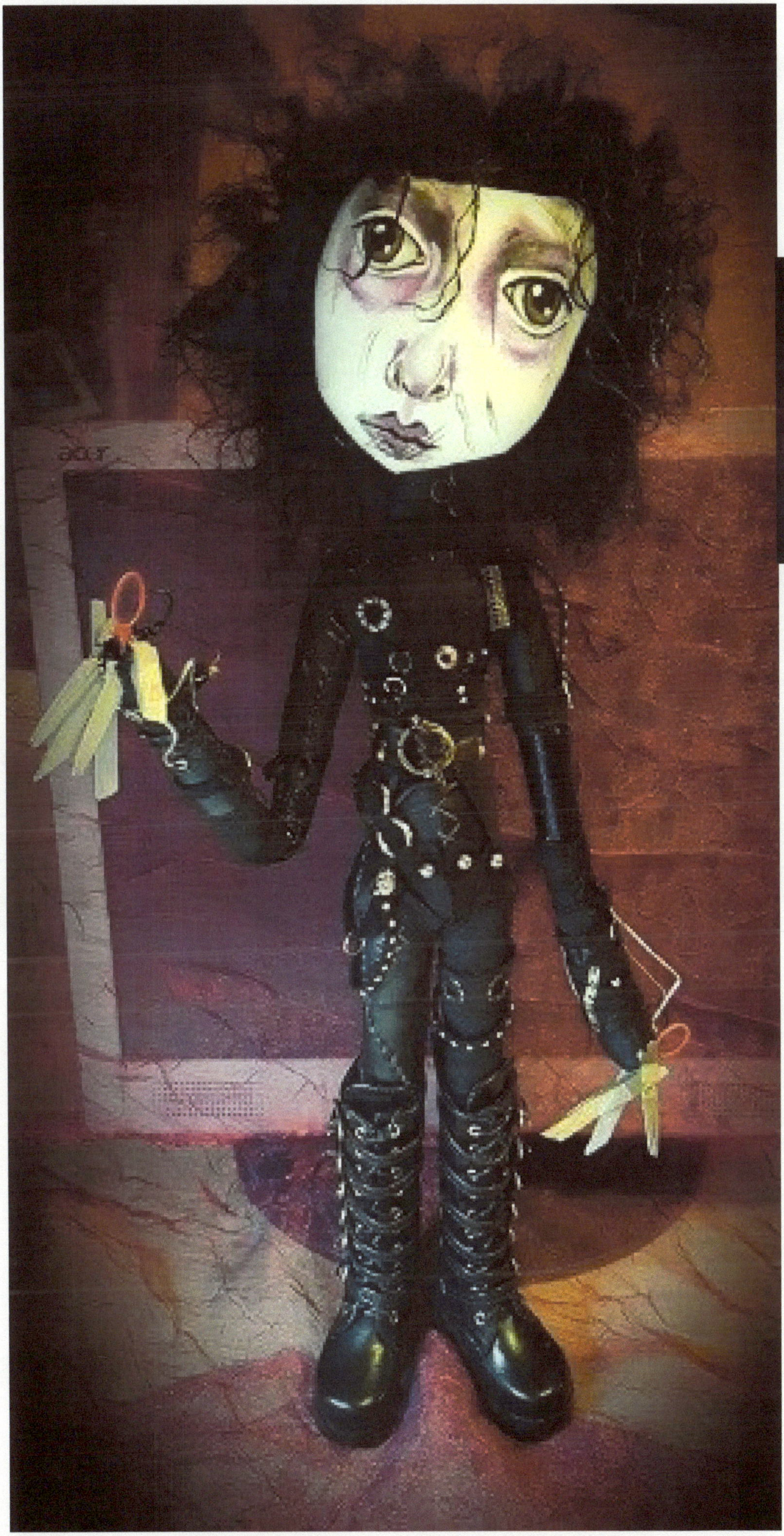

Edward Sissorhands

By Louise Crone

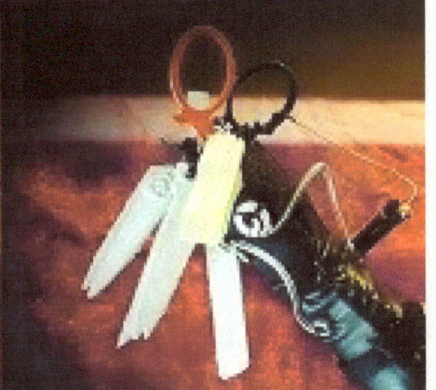

Louise Crone is from Australia. She hand makes cloth art dolls with some mixed media. We present Edward Scissorhands. Apart from his boots, his costume is fully hand made. He stands 45cms (17.75") tall and his face is hand painted.

Louise Crone

Carma Enchanted Dolls

Carmaenchanted

@gmail.com

Constructing a Corset for Your Doll

by Kori Leppart

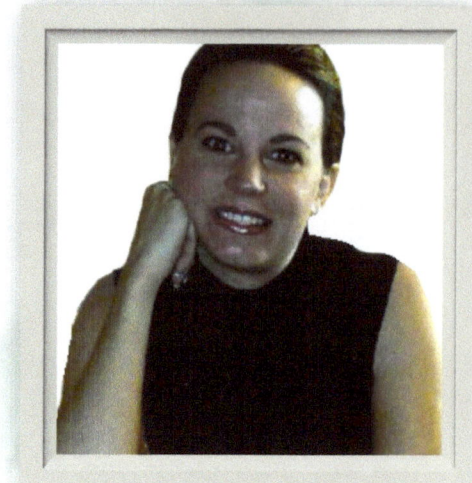

IT IS IMPORTANT TO GET A GOOD FIT when constructing a corset for your doll. To begin wrap your doll's torso closely with plastic wrap. Secure it with scotch tape. Repeat wrapping the torso so that you have two layers of cellophane to protect your doll.

Using duct tape of a light color start taping around your doll's torso. This tape will be the base for your pattern. Once you have your doll completely wrapped with tape, tape another length across the center of the torso to get a tight fit on the waist. With a sharpie pen, start marking the pattern lines on the duct tape. When doing this try to keep your marks even on both sides.

Carefully cut the duct tape form off your doll. Starting from the split line up the center back and cut between the layers of cellophane. You should have **one layer of cellophane stuck** to the duct tape and another still secured around the doll's torso.
Now cut the pattern pieces apart. These forms are the shapes you will use for drafting your corset pattern. I use pattern webbing, which you can purchase from a fabric store. You can also just use tissue paper. Using the duct tape forms, draw out the pattern shapes. You really only need to use one side of your cut pieces including the front piece, as you can alternate them for the pattern pieces for the opposite side. Add 1/4 inch around each piece for seam allowance. I also mark my lines at this time where I would like my boning to be.

Cut the pattern pieces from your front facing fabric, cut one set of pieces out of your lining fabric and another set out of your heavy duty fusible web.
Iron the heavy duty interfacing to the front fabric pieces. Sew together all the front fabric pieces, then the lining pieces. Pin the front pieced fabric to the lining, with **seams matched up.** Line the edges up.

Stitch over the seam lines, what is referred to as "stitching in the ditch". You will also be top stitching all the boning channels at this time. Insert the boning once the channels are sewn. Sewing the corset like this will leave the outer edges raw. These you will want to bind these using a coordinating hem tape or ribbon if you prefer. I prefer to hand stitch the hem tape for a finished look.

To finish the corset, bind all the raw edges with hem tape. Attach an even amount of eyelets on each side of the back edges. You may also want to add a modesty panel behind where the corset lines up. Decorate

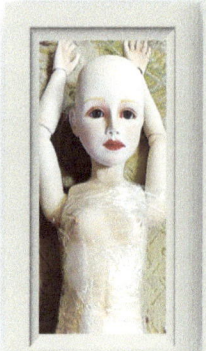
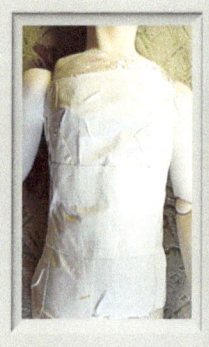
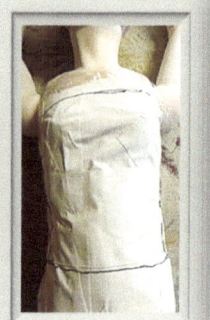
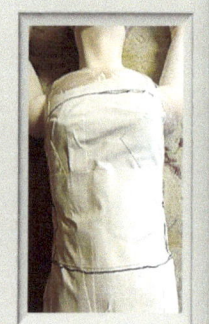
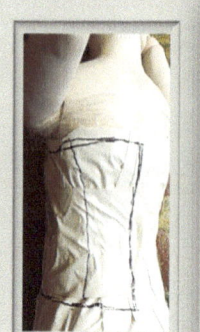
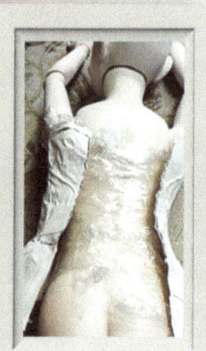

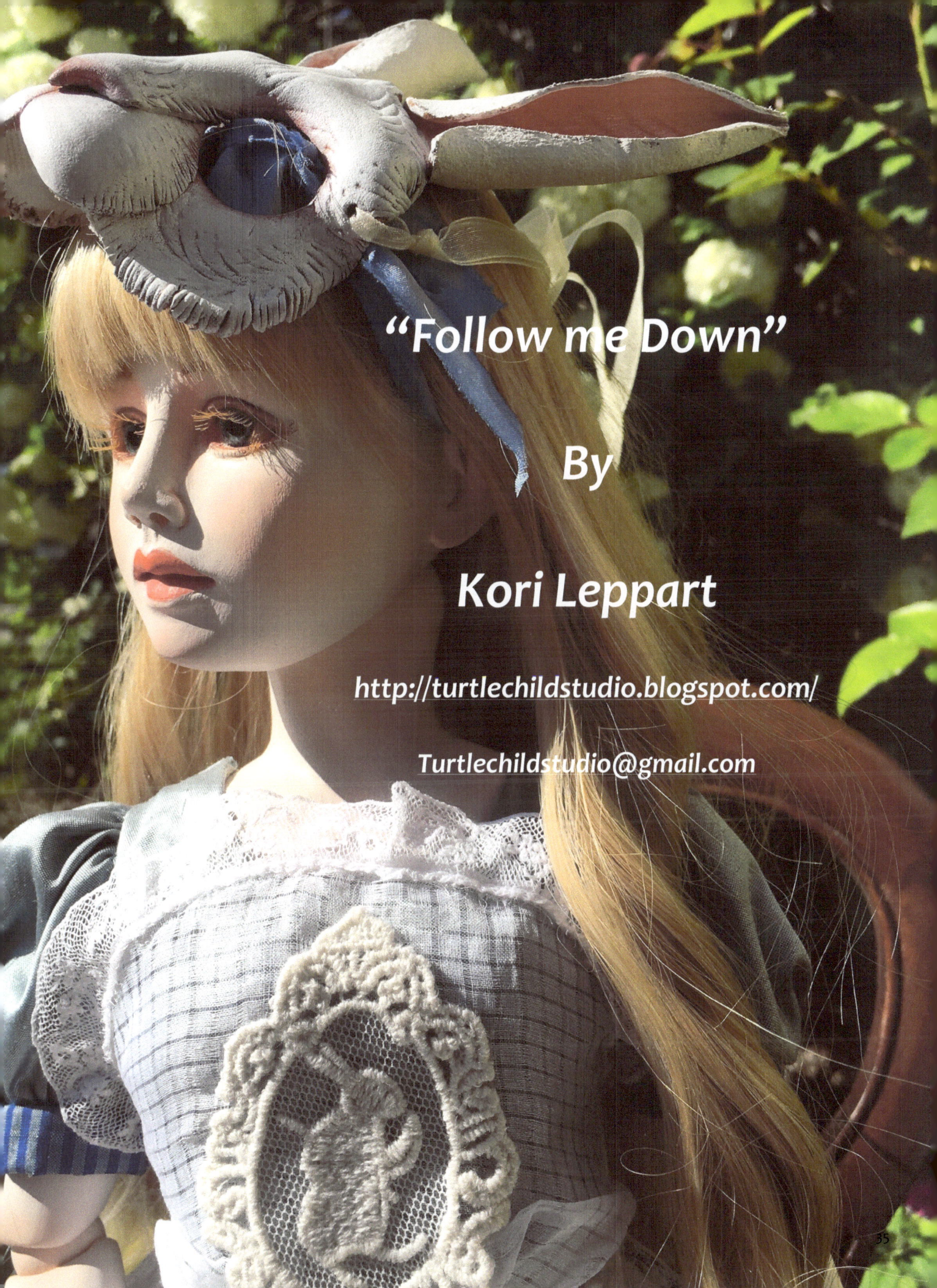

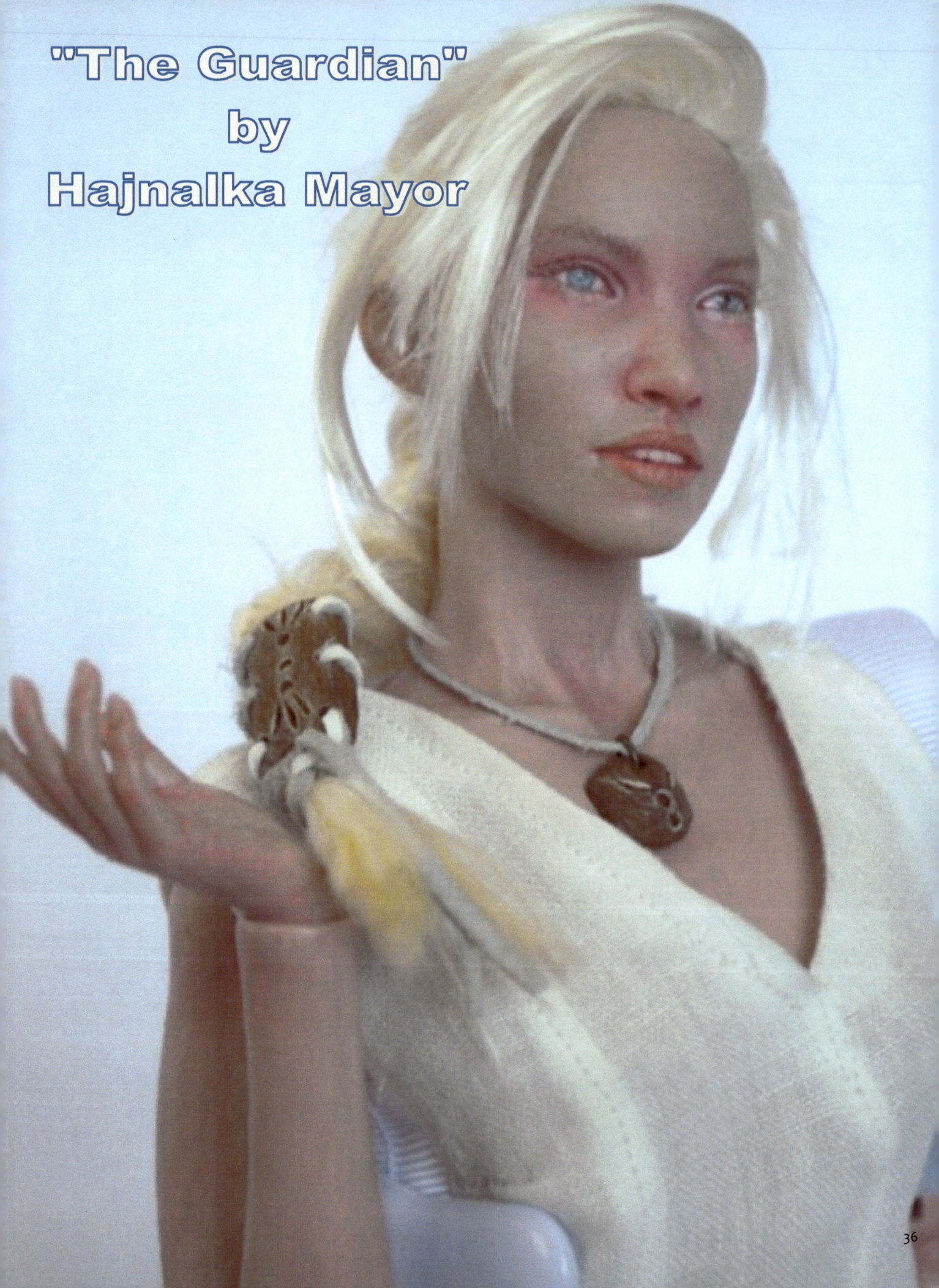

"The Guardian" by Hajnalka Mayor

"The Guardian" by Hajnalka Mayor

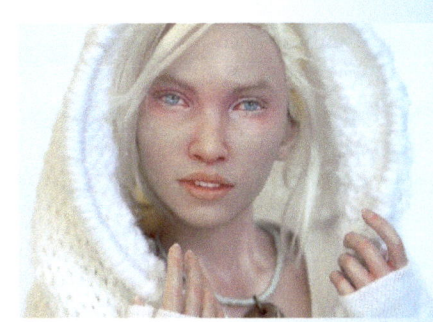

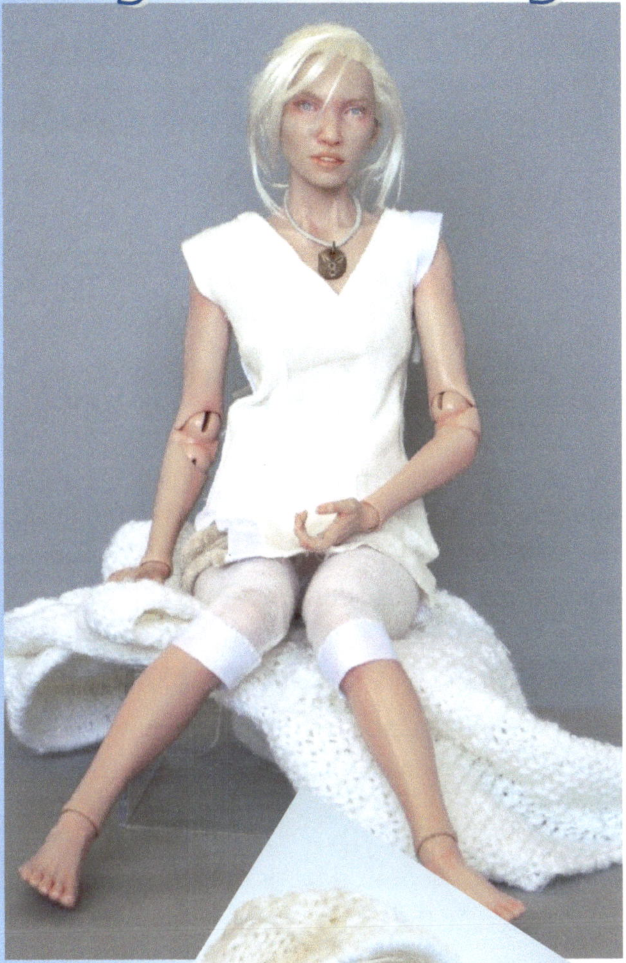

"The guardian" is an OOAK BJD doll, sculpted from polymer clay. She stands 15.5 in tall.

She is a celestial/ angelic being, a member of a guardian species. I wanted to make her look eternal yet modern. She has very pale skin, icy blue eyes framed with blond eyelashes, attached one by one, and white - blond hair. Her hair is made from an alpaca - viscose blend. I glued it in very thin rows directly to the head, and before the glue dried, I used a metal tool to arrange the hair in a more natural looking order. I wanted her hair style to be practical and a little messy. So she has a simple braiding with several shorter hair pieces escaping from it. For her outfit I used several different fabrics and mediums. As a reference, I used fashion pictures related to futuristic and post apocalyptic style. Her leggings are made from very thin cotton with silk ribbon on the knees. I used the same fabric for her half gloves as well. Her dress is made from stripes sewed together following an asymmetric line. I used linen, velvet and silk ribbon. It has two long zips in it, one on the back and one on the left side.
I hand knitted her coat, and I kind of made up the pattern as I went on. The hood has a fish bone support which results a nice futuristic look.
For her hair piece, necklace and the button I used drift wood and leather. I carved the same pattern into all the accessories. Drift wood is a wonderful carving medium, I will definitely use it more in the future.

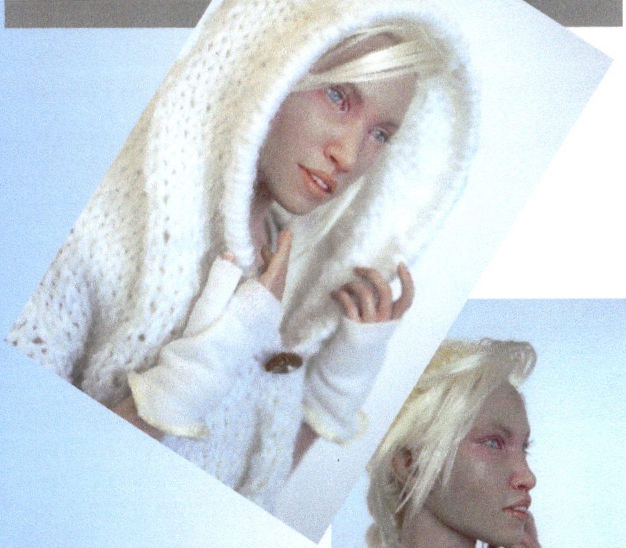

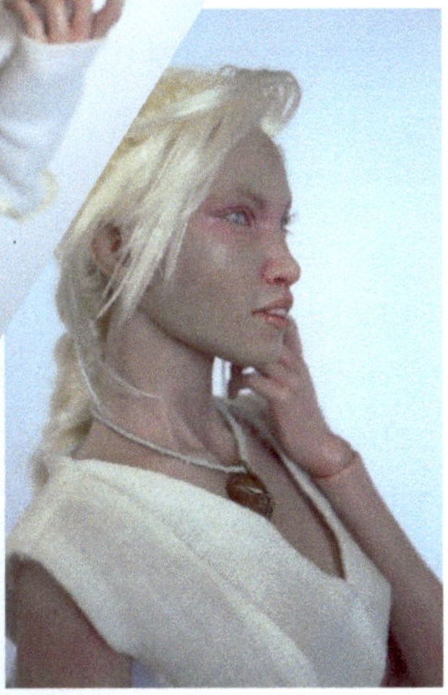

About the doll: I wanted to give her a pair of cozy winter boots. I used two layers of tooling leather for the soles. At the front and at the heels I put a piece of thinner leather for support. The nose is covered with a thin layer of cotton fabric than painted with acrylic paint. The rest of the upper part is made from two layers, a simple cotton fabric inside, and a thick knitted cotton outside.
One of the reasons I started to make ball jointed dolls is the opportunity to challenge my inner fashion design.

Hajnalka Mayor

New Zealand, Wellington
www.hajnalkasfantasyart.com
https://www.facebook.com/hajnalkasfantasyart

hajnalkasfantasyart@gmail.com

Costuming

ENDLESS POSSIBILITIES

By LISA WROBLEWSKI

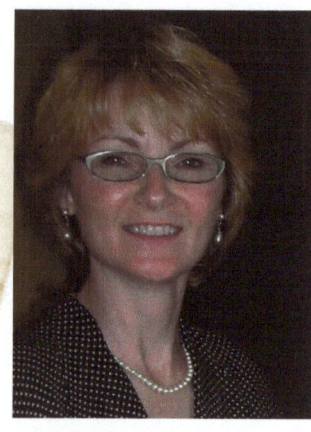

It's all about the details.

Costuming of your art doll is as important as sculpting the doll itself. As doll artists, we spend many hours refining our creations and when it comes time to embellish the final piece, we sometimes fall short. It's easier than you think to use your imagination to detailing the costume as well.

Having the right scale is the essential element to achieve a more realistic look. There are several ways to assemble the fabrics, trims and embellishments.

Two widely used costuming methods are sewing or applied. Sewing requires the skill of using a machine or meticulous use of a needle and thread. Applied refers to the use of adhesives which come in various options. You can combine the methods on your piece and drape fabrics and trims or place adornments directly to the sculpture with adhesive to reduce the bulk of folded seams. Selecting the weight (thickness) of your fabrics, trims and embellishments needs to be considered thoughtfully to match the sculpture's personality. Some of the best options for lightweight fabrics are silks, sheers, cottons, knits and gauze. Just be sure to match the scale of the pattern to the size of your project.

Depending on the style and type of sculpture you're working with such as stationary, ball jointed, or dolls for play, you can gather your materials from many sources and don't have to just rely on fabrics alone. You're already creative, think outside the box and stretch your imagination to create the vision of a professional costume. Be expressive and let your thoughts explore the many possibilities.

Think beyond fabric stores and shop your local discount and thrift shops for children's socks, tights and undergarments which are perfect for dolls as they have tiny prints available and are lightweight with a little stretch for a perfect fit for those petite pieces.

Your local flea markets and antique stores have a bountiful display of trinkets and treasures. So does your hardware store with various doodads and gadgets that are ideal for steampunk styles. Start with the vision and open your mind, before you know it you will be so excited to have found that perfect item that's going to bring it all together.

Endless Possibilities

Search for ribbons, trims and laces which have finished edges or are gathered for an easy transition from a selection of fabric. Adding finer textures onto the sculpt allows you to create a delicate look and add more layers to create a fuller design. Natural decorative or textured papers may also be incorporated to add an organic look. Silk flowers, leaves, butterfly wings, acorn tops…. the list is endless. Creating tiny hats and dresses is my favorite way to embellish with these and I reserve my best natural materials for my fairies.

Costuming continued

Enhancing these items with paint, glitter and beads gives you endless possibilities to create your unique vision. Fabrics and ribbons can also be cut into flower and petal shapes to use as is, fray the edges, or apply glue and glitter to keep from fraying then apply directly to your sculpture as part of your costume. Use petals cut from tulle in between your other petals and a tulle underskirt for added fullness. Use of tulle and cheesecloth in my designs are another favorite with no hem required and they are inexpensive!

Vintage Treasures

My favorite items to collect are vintage, they are made with quality unlike modern pieces and are a great way to repurpose too. You can find these treasures at flea markets, thrift stores, garage sales and antique shops. I love to reuse things I already have or to score that perfect item while antique shopping! Keep your eyes open for these items:

What is more perfect than doll clothes? You can always embellish and make it your own, but also great for re-working or disassemble for the fabric, trim and buttons as they are already the perfect weight and scale. Many doll shows, flea markets and garage sales sell vintage doll clothes at a bargain price.

Santa isn't Santa without his soft, fluffy trim. Repurpose fur coats and scarves (real or faux) for Santa trim or a teddy bear or a bunny rabbit.

You can reuse costume jewelry pieces and beads which are wonderful for creating jewelry for your dolls or sewing or applying the jewels onto your sculpture or costume. Tiny doll buttons and buckles are difficult to source now with the quality of vintage and are gems when you can find them.

An often overlooked material is used leather gloves that are thin, soft and worn. They are the basis for the best looking shoes, boots and hats.

Delicate linens, chiffon scarves, handkerchiefs, laces and trims are delicate and have amazing embroidery and detailed designs perfect to use as a dress or pinafore.

Think outside the box when you are selecting pieces for your costuming project. Open your mind to the abundance that surrounds you. The possibilities are truly endless. Happy creating!

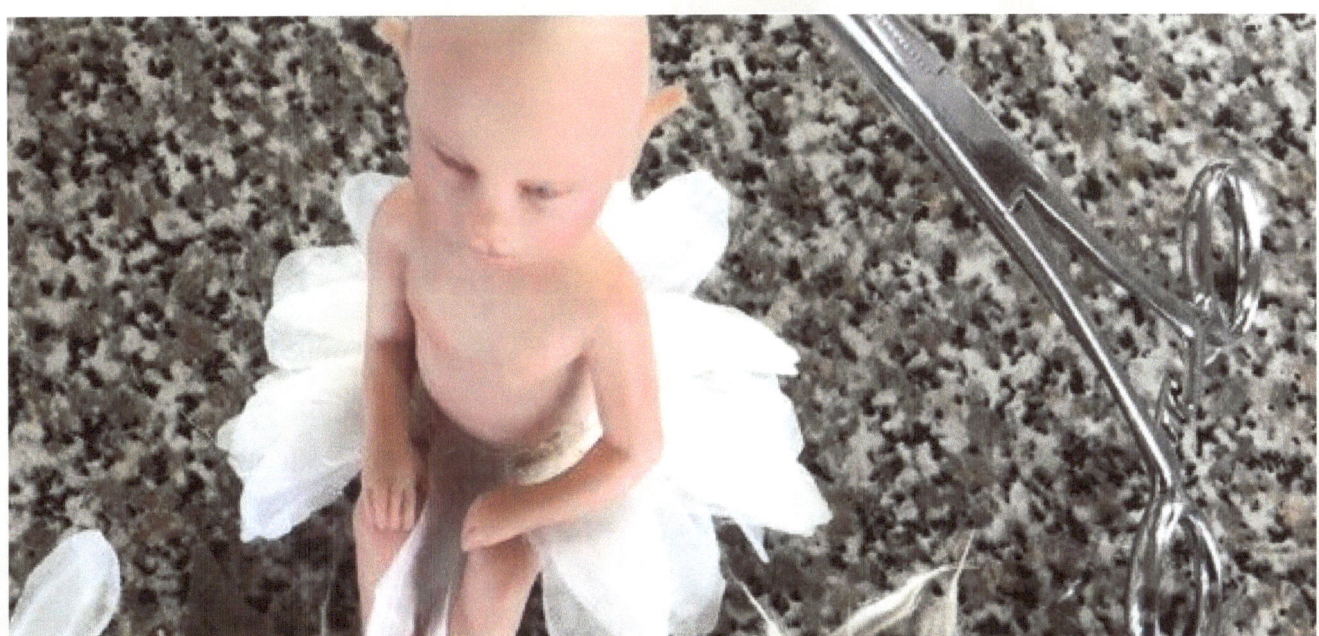

Costuming ...continued

OUTSIDE THE BOX

1. FLOWERS

Create simple flower hats by using a flower turned upside down.

2. TRIMS

Trims applied with glue directly onto the sculpt can create the look of fabric.

3. PETALS

Flower petals cut from ribbon and fabric are applied in layers with glue directly onto the body to form a skirt.

4. ACORNS

A dried acorn can become a quick and simple fairy hat.

5. RIBBONS

Ribbons can be placed onto your doll for a softer finished look.

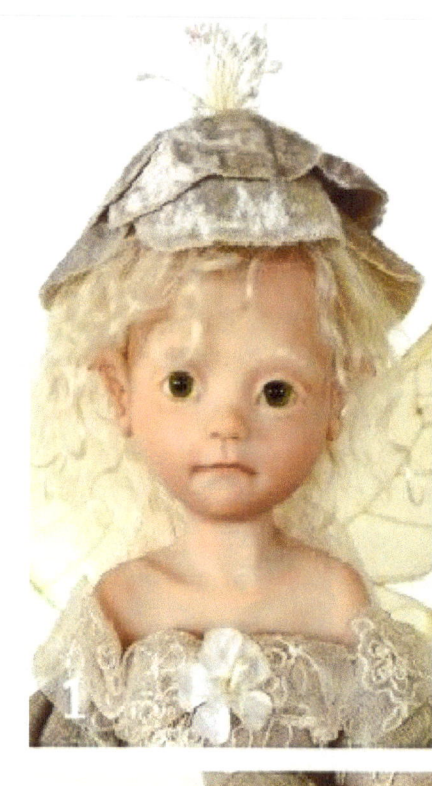
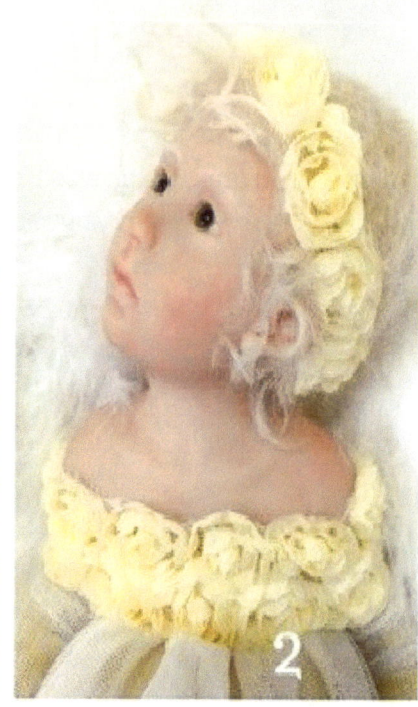
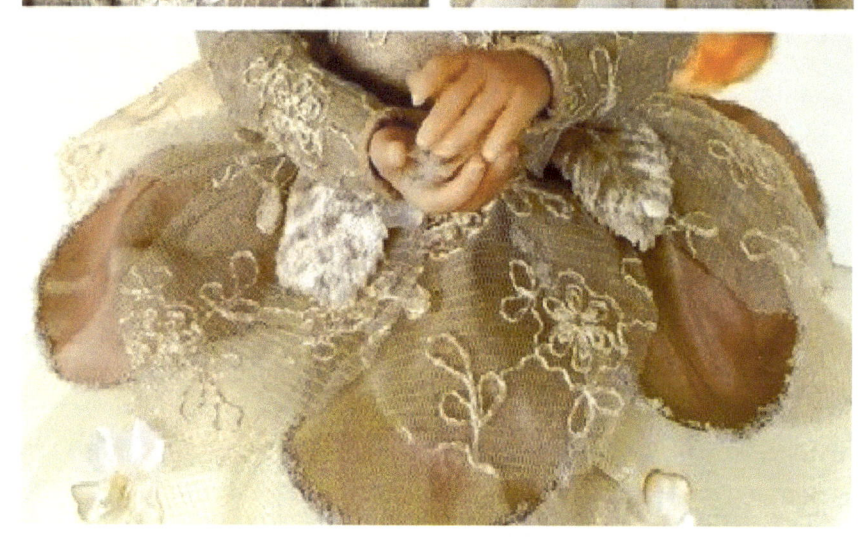

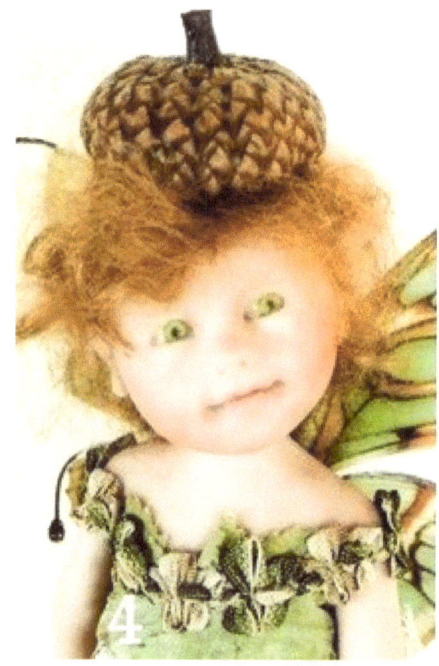
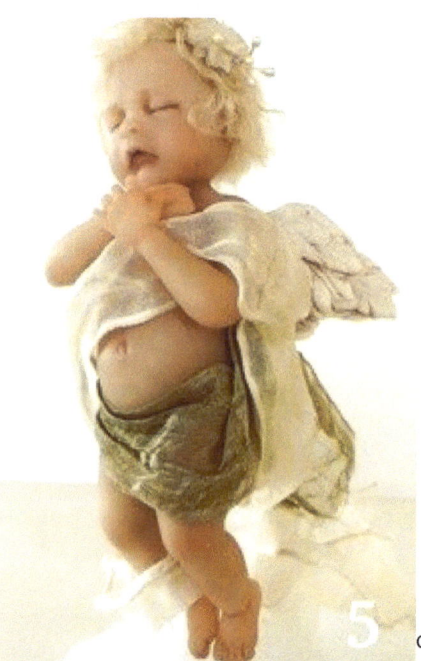

Costuming ...continued
OUTSIDE THE BOX

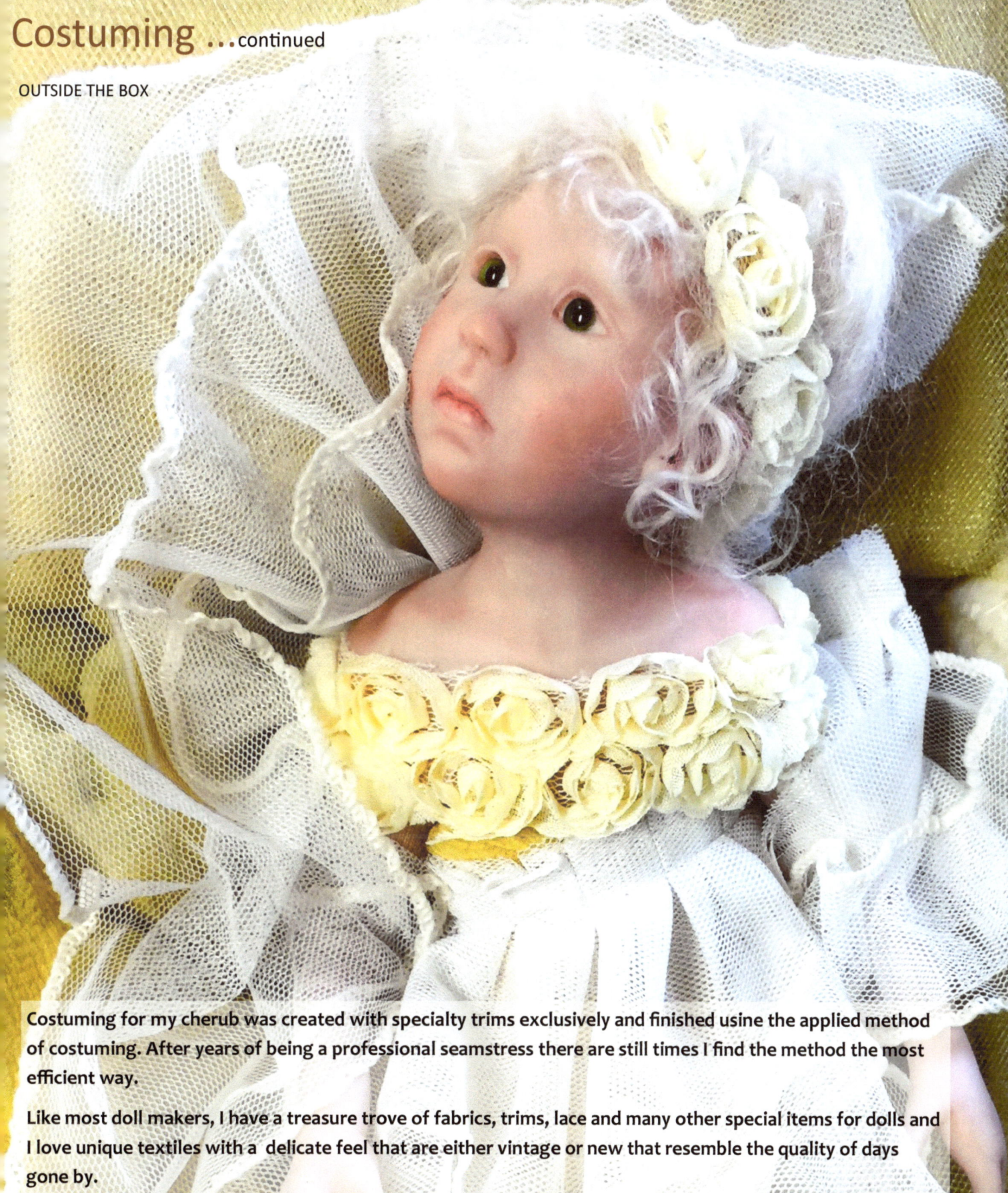

Costuming for my cherub was created with specialty trims exclusively and finished usine the applied method of costuming. After years of being a professional seamstress there are still times I find the method the most efficient way.

Like most doll makers, I have a treasure trove of fabrics, trims, lace and many other special items for dolls and I love unique textiles with a delicate feel that are either vintage or new that resemble the quality of days gone by.

You can see my work on my website at: https://cecilandco.com/ where you will find figurative art dolls, fairy wings, tutorials, doll supplies and vintage treasures.

Trending in the Industry.

by Linda Ehrenfried

Human Movement Dolls

There is a new trend starting in the art doll industry and it is all about the armature. Gaining in popularity with each new artist who dares to try them these previously hard to come by armature parts are quickly becoming a favorite. The dolls featured are very pose-able, and showcase the fantastic costuming skills of Artist and Entrepreneur Natasha Nazarova of Morezmore Studio. These stop motion style armatures are sweeping their way into the hearts of artists and collectors a like. Giving their creations and collections the ability to pose like never before. As part of her venture into using these armatures herself Natasha also procured the parts for the armatures to sell in her online shop as kits complete with all you need to create your own at a very reasonable rate.

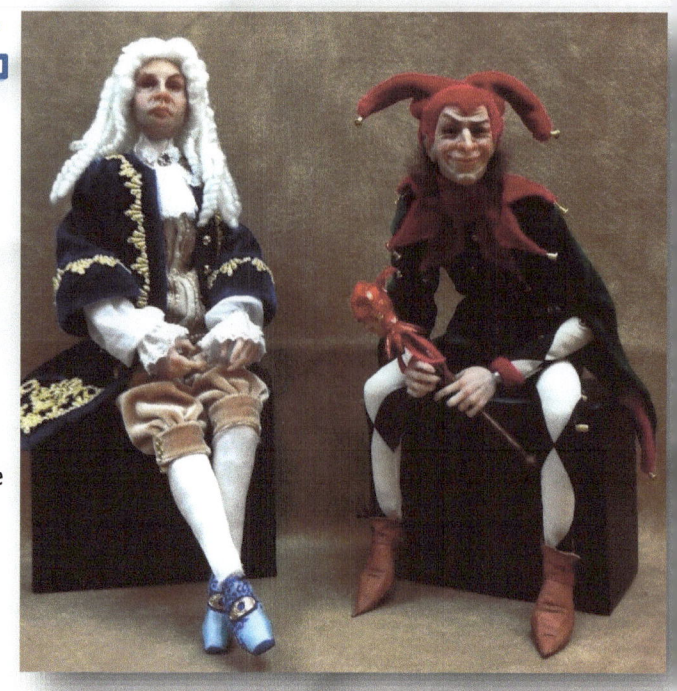

Natasha's Creations

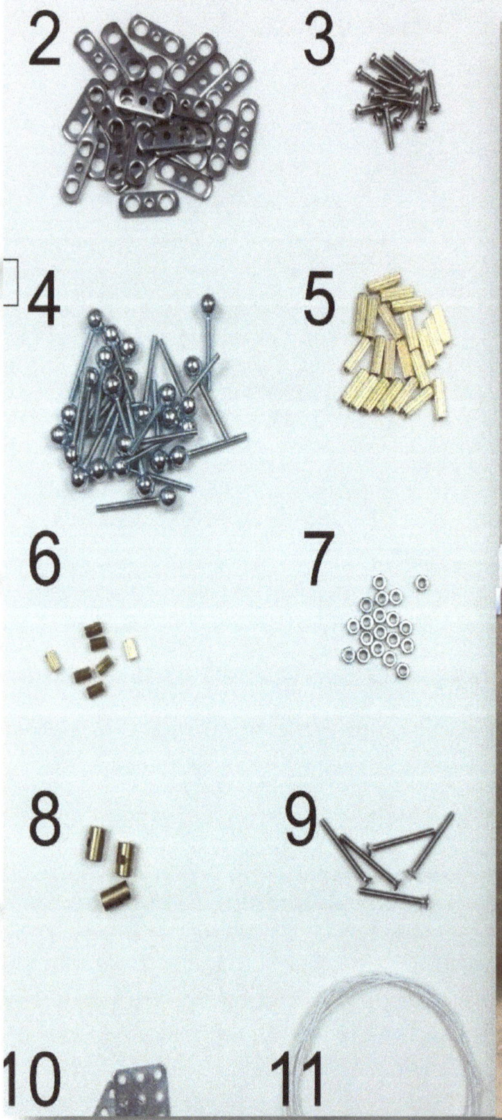

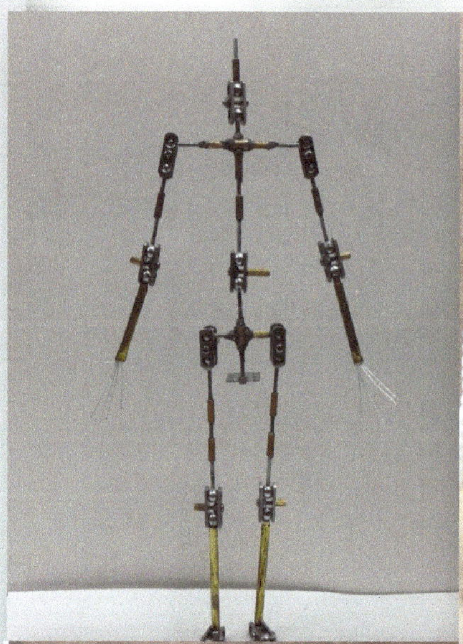

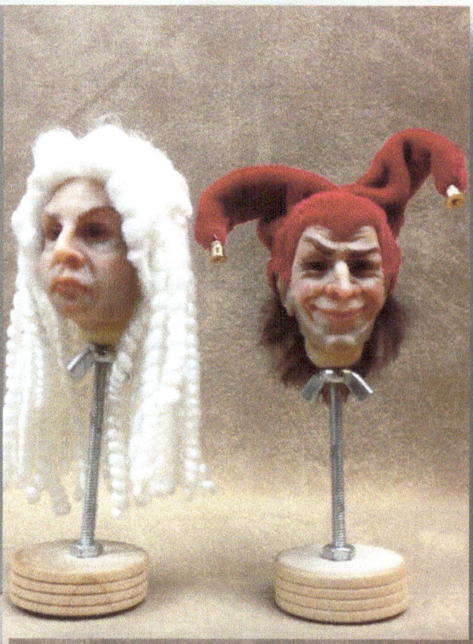

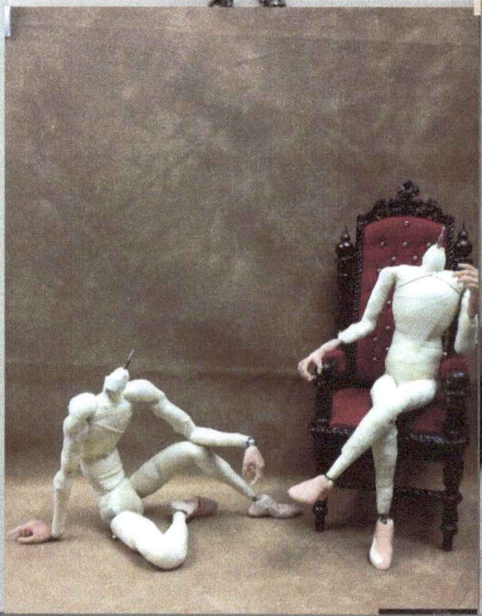

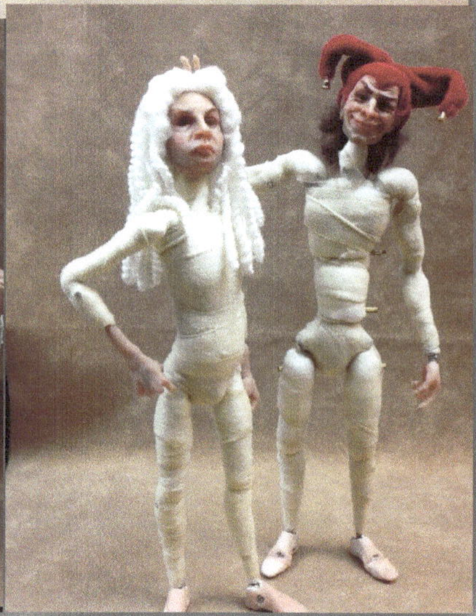

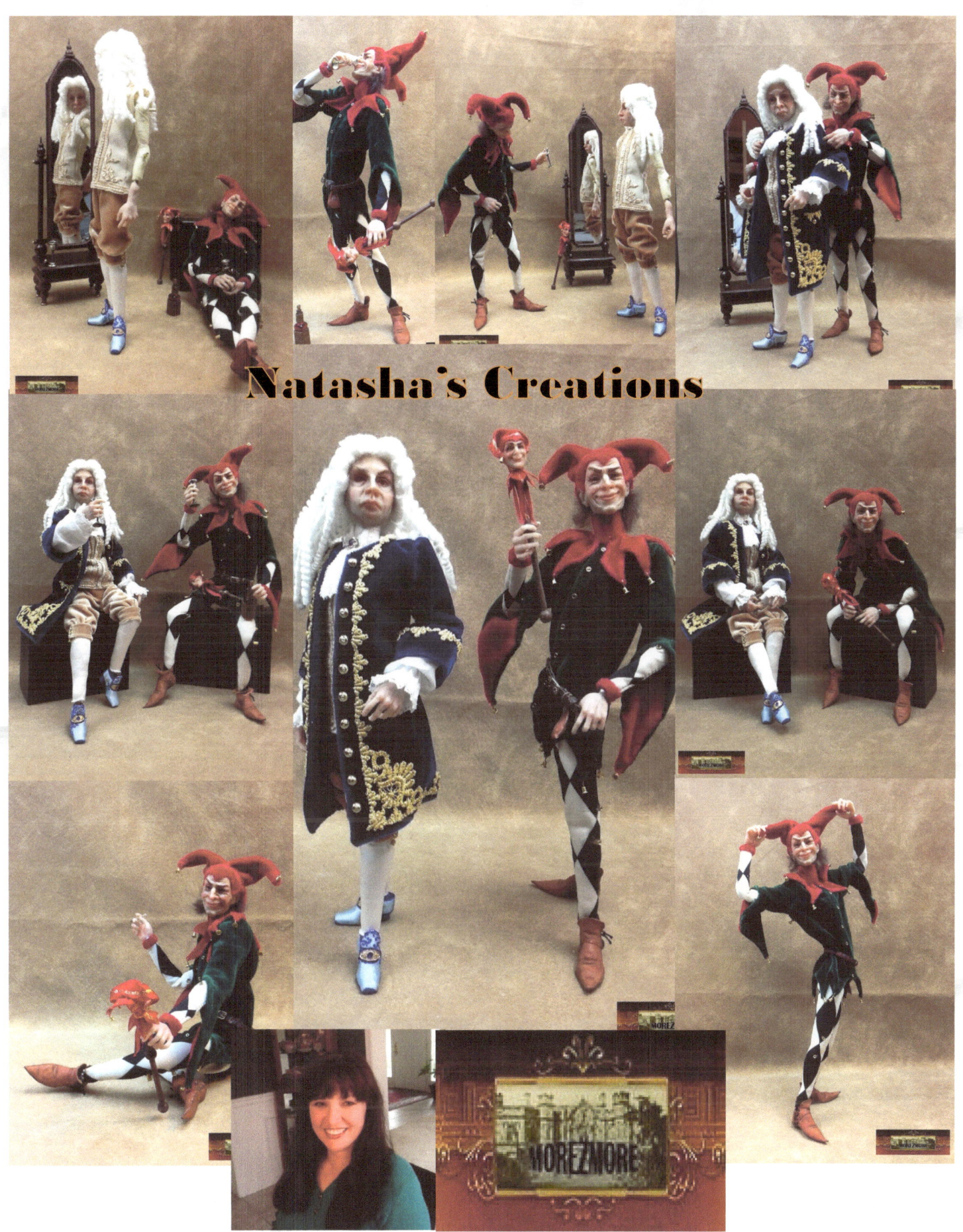

Natasha's Creations

Contact Natasha at creator@morezmore.com

"The Red Shoes"
by Ioanna Paraskeva

The Doll was inspired from the movie "The Red Shoes" and represents the emotional fight when you have to select between two things that you love the most and that you need the most in order to be happy and balanced.

joartdolls@gmail.com

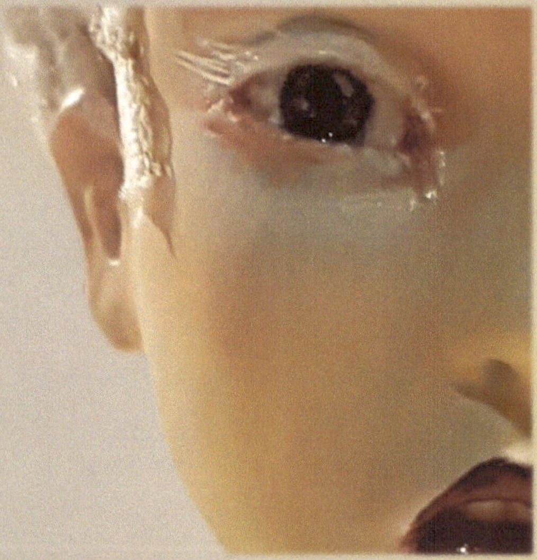

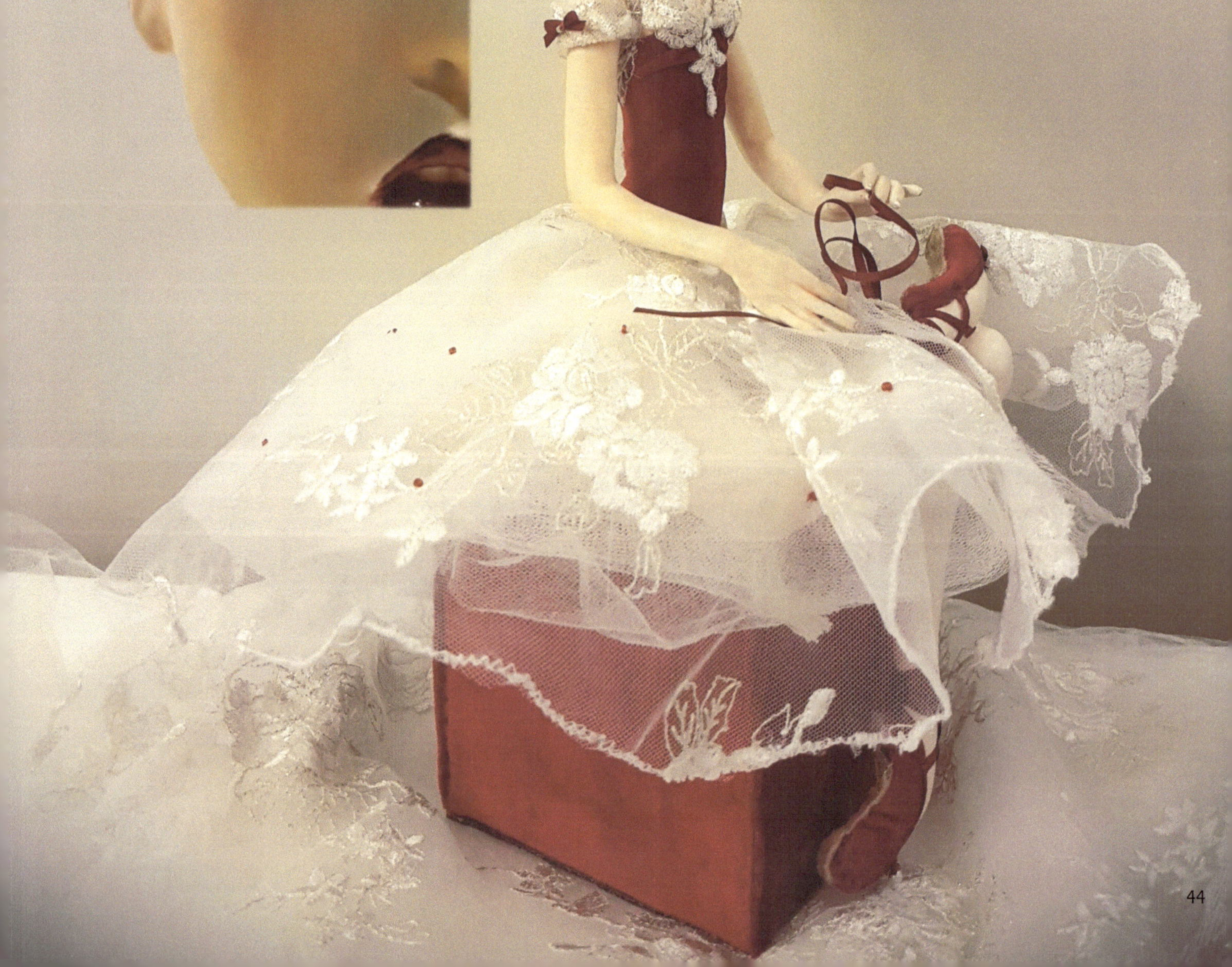

Christmas Gallery

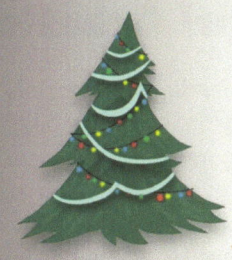

"Wind's Knee's"
by Lindsay Cough
www.facebook.com/WindsKnees

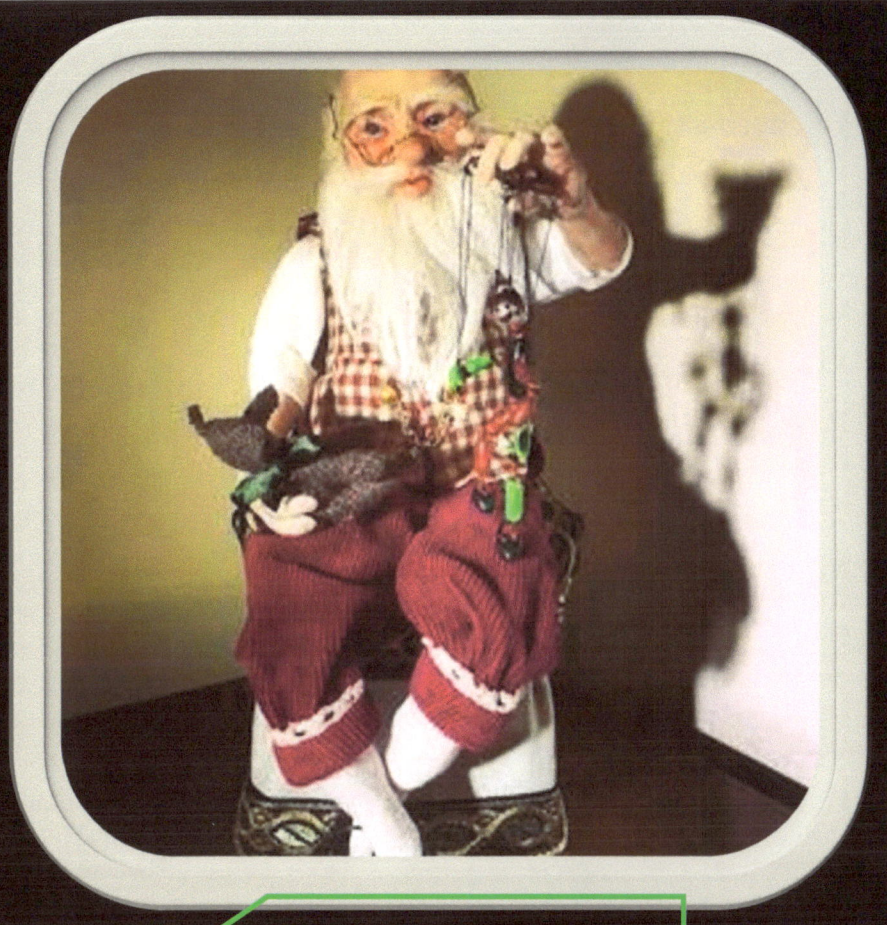

Smiling Santa
By Tracey Donop
Tdonoporiginals@aol.com

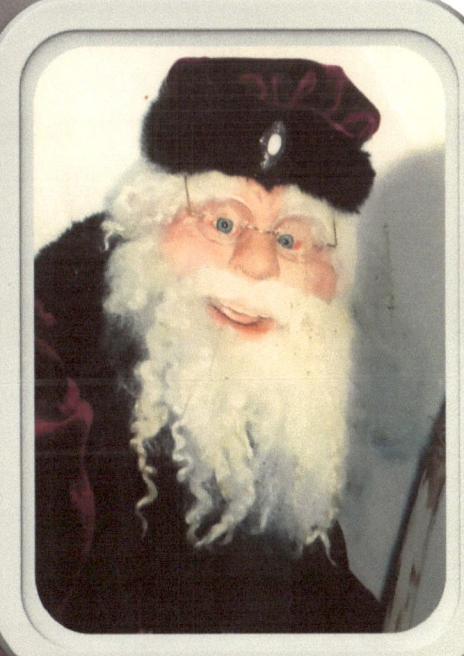

"Santa is building a Snowman"
by Patricia Davis
craftypat2004@gmail.com

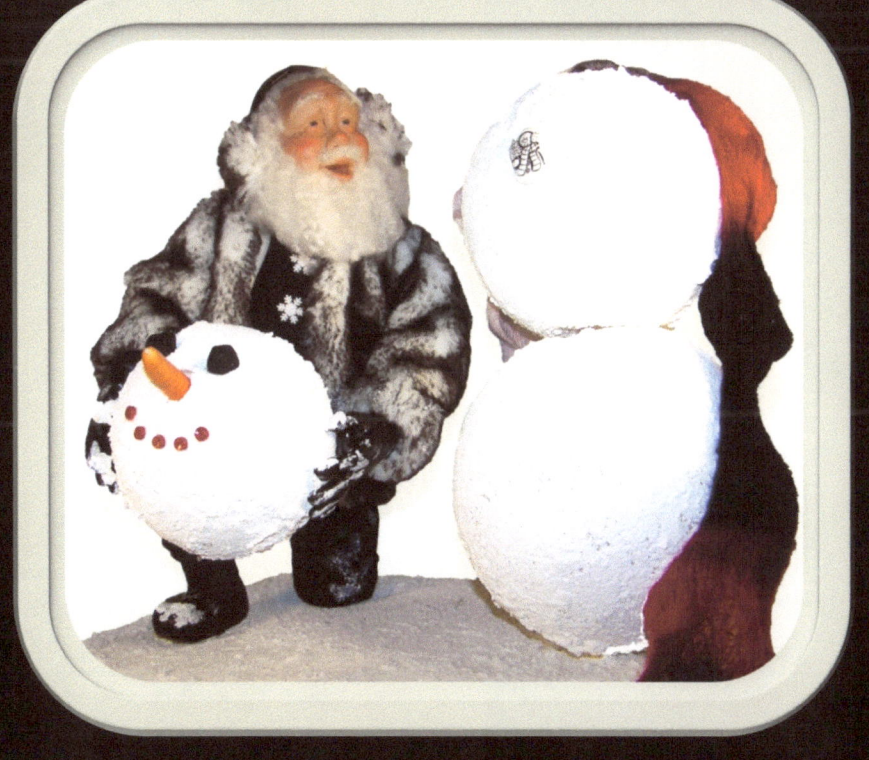

Here Comes Santa

**"Stormy"
by
Cherie Davidson
Darlin Girl Creations**

This is my first human figure wool doll. The one that got me started ion sculptural needle felting of art dolls so he has a special place in my heart and will forever be in my personal collection. I don't have any of the sculptural wool art dolls I've created, since they've been for commissions or gifts, but this little guy, my first, has a prominent place in my studio! He is 100% wool, needle felted from wool batts. No armature. He stands without needing support, and he's completely hand needled by me, and OOAK. He took me about three weeks to complete. I modeled him after the ultimate Santa Clause of my childhood, the one I always imagined in my mind's eye and just knew was the one leaving me presents when I was five and six years old. I smiled the entire time I was needling him to life!

His clothing was also needle felted from fluffy wool batting. I felted the red coat directly on to the body, except where the cuffs, and hem of coat, are. They needed to have more dimension, so I used multiple needles.

Santa's Secret

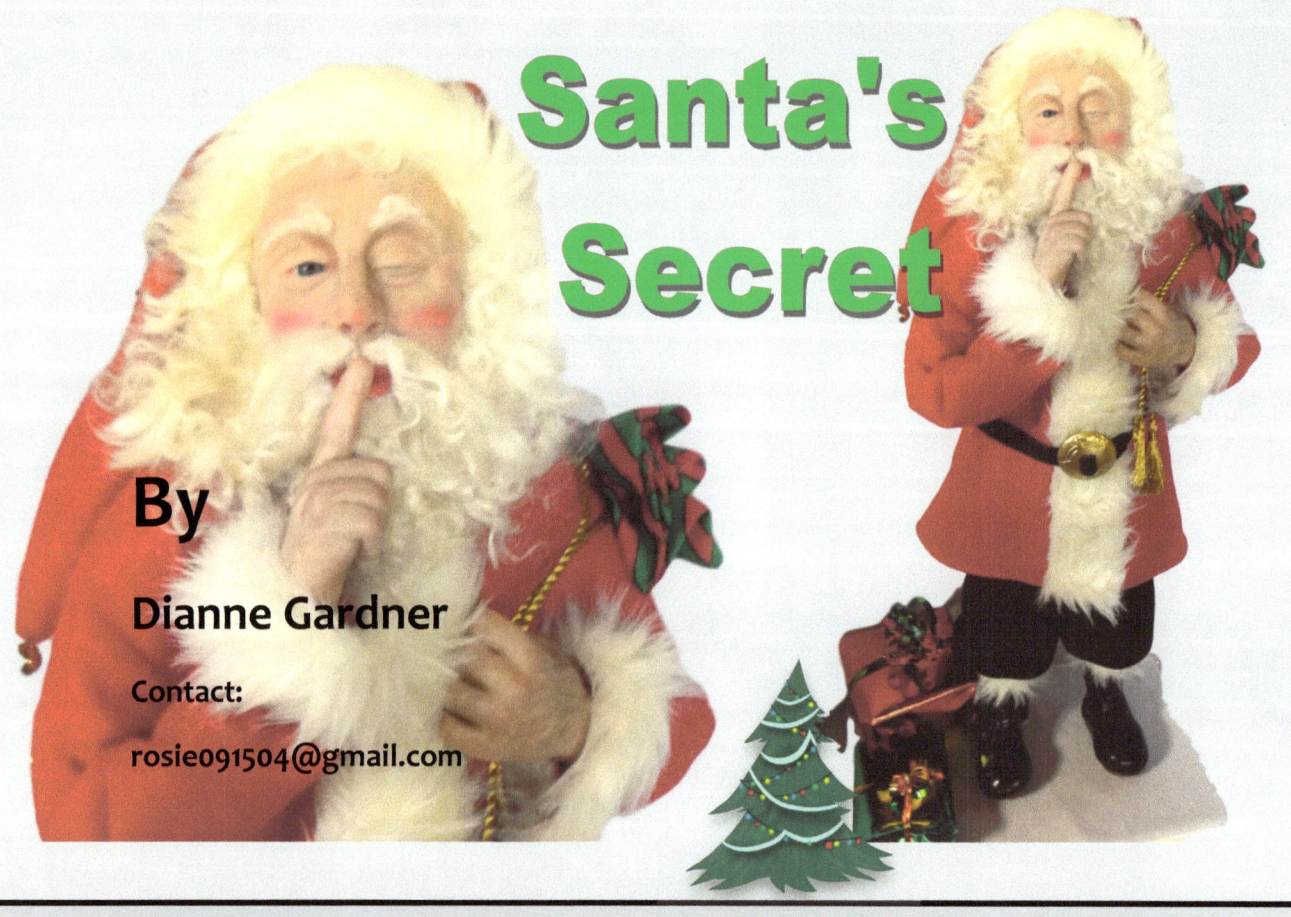

By

Dianne Gardner

Contact:

rosie091504@gmail.com

Skating Lessons

By Melinda Wood

mindysfairies@comcast.net

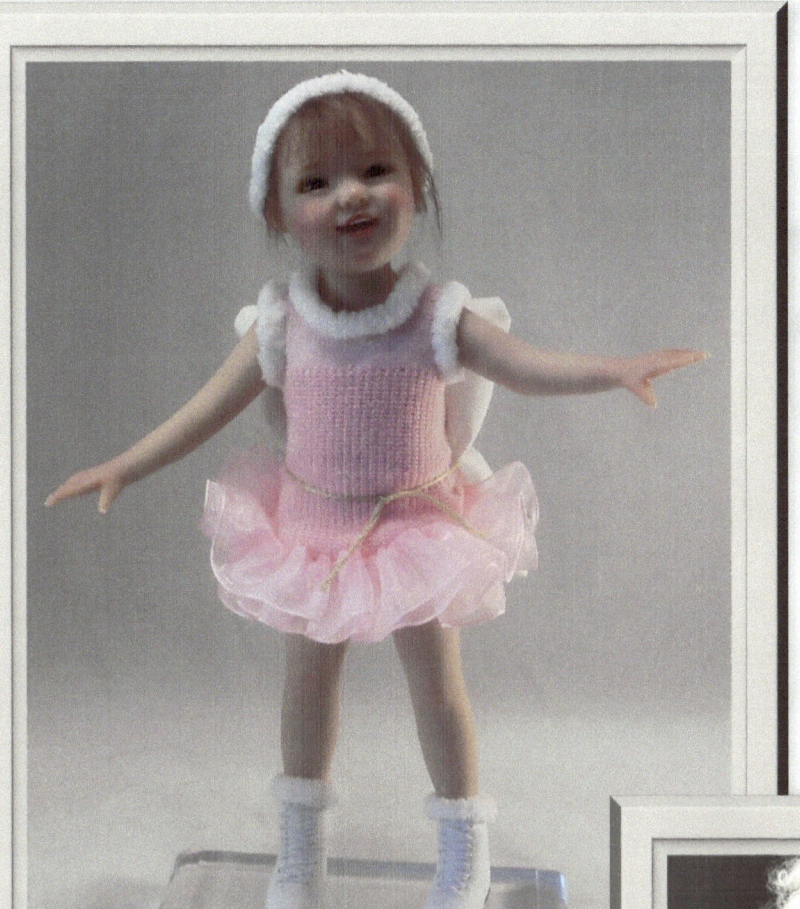

Santa Lucia
by Alessandra Nicolin

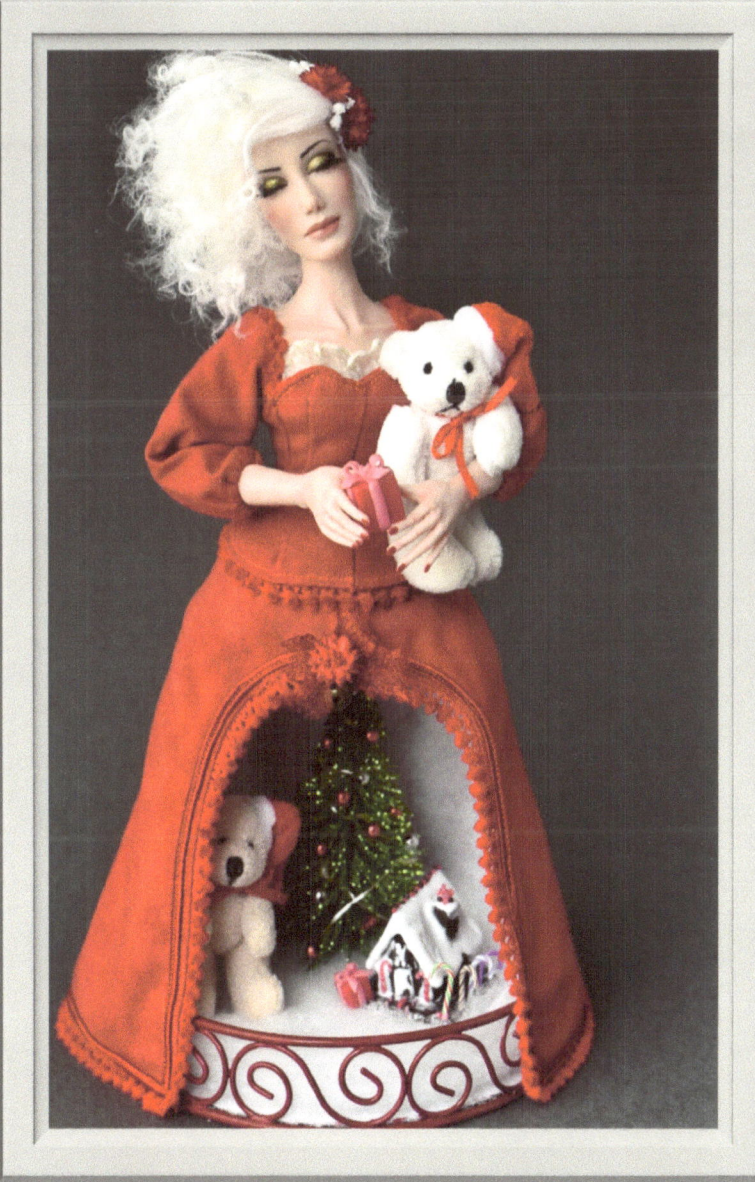

Christmas is usually linked to Santa Claus and its businesses to deliver gifts to children. In many countries in northern Italy and northern Europe, Instead, Santa Lucia has the sights of Santa Claus; the day when Santa Lucia is celebrated is December 13th and linked to her very particular traditions and legends. She has her arms moving to hold the bears and the gifts to give. Under her skirt, Alessandra made a scene with the Christmas tree that lights up with a small switch behind her skirt. The marzipan house and the gift are made by her in polymer clay. Santa Lucia is about 10 inches tall.

Contact: alessandra.nicolin@gmail.com

Learning to Sculpt...

Introducing....... Elfie Vacation.

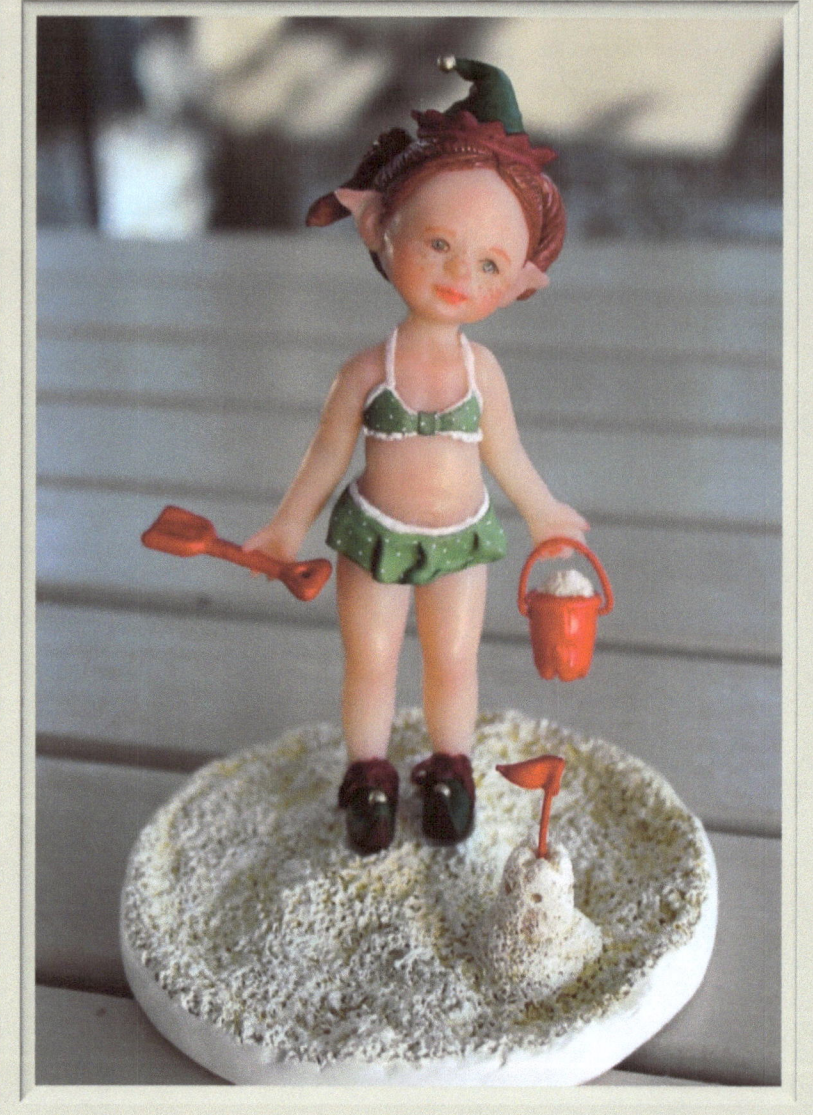

Elfie is a little Christmas elf who has opted out of the festivities this year - instead she is enjoying some R&R time at the beach! This piece gives us a glimpse into her day as she has fun building sandcastles with her spade and sand bucket. From the look on her face, she may be a little bit wistful because as much fun as she's having, she still misses her home and the work that she so loves.

About the doll: Elfie Vacation is a fully sculpted work, from the doll herself to all of her clothing, shoes, accessories, stand and hair. The piece is around six inches (including the base) and has an invisible stand so the doll may be removed. Elfie's hands are capable of holding her removable bucket and spade. She has been blushed using pastels and painted with acrylic paint. I also used a little mica powder for sparkle, alcohol ink for the bells on her shoes and hat, and gloss to add shine. The sand is also sculpted, colored with pastels, acrylic paint and a little gloss here and there.

About the artist: Deborah Randall is a busy mum and artist living in Perth, Western Australia. She has eight children from the ages of 3 years old to 15 years old. She has been sculpting for just over a year and is currently an apprentice in the Professional Doll Makers Art Guild Academy. She lives to create, and can hardly even sit still without something for her hands to work on. She is hoping that one day she will be able to help our family financially by selling her work and teaching others to do what she can do.

Deborah Randall

Naughtydebbers@hotmail.com

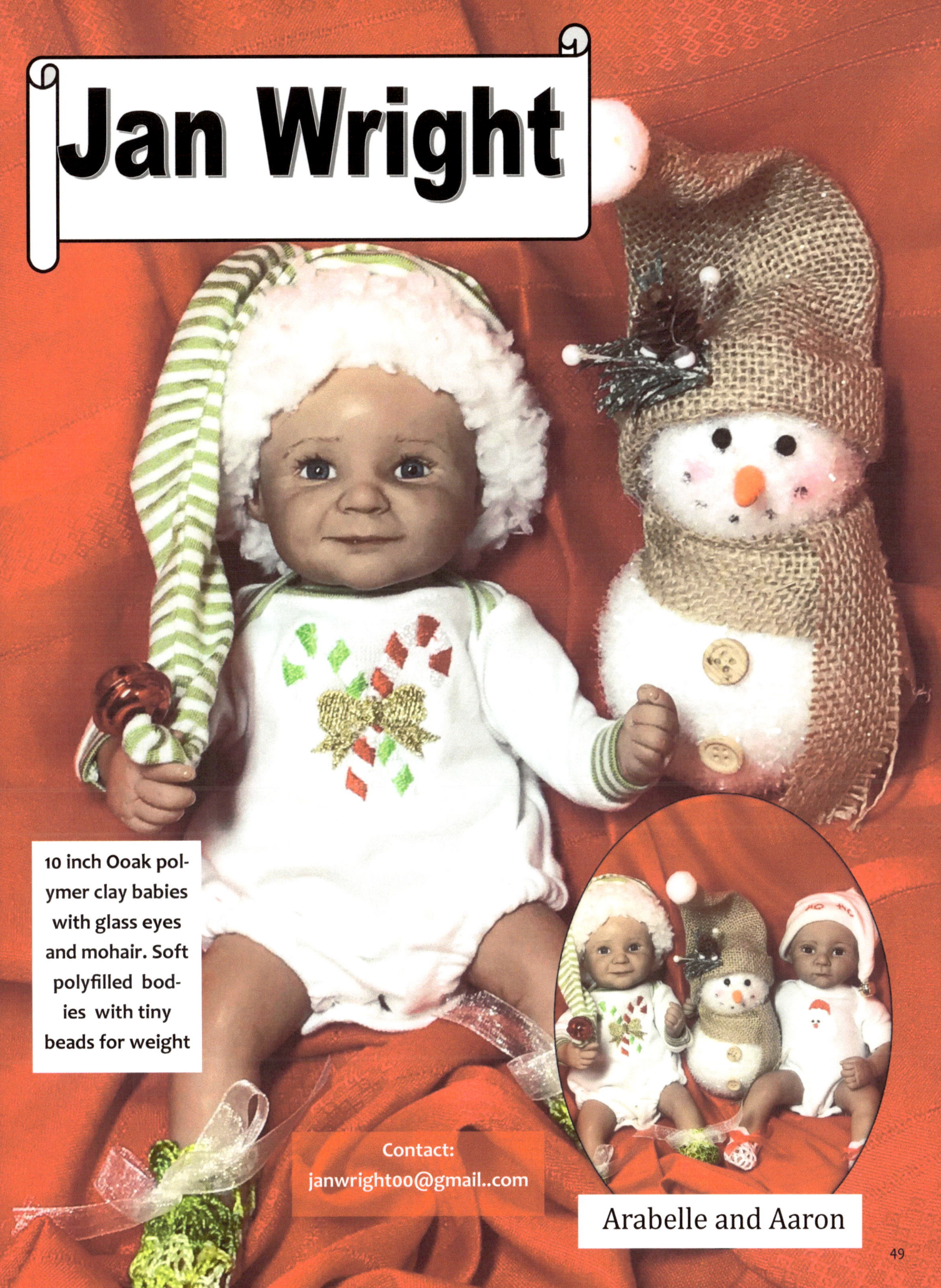

Jan Wright

10 inch Ooak polymer clay babies with glass eyes and mohair. Soft polyfilled bodies with tiny beads for weight

Contact: janwright00@gmail..com

Arabelle and Aaron

Augustus the Earl of Grey, How an artist made porcelain

Meet the latest member in the Realm of Wymsy. Our one-of-a-kind hand crafted porcelain doll creation is an impoverished Earl. The only remaining portion of his dwindling fortune is the village newspaper, *The Bellwether*, which he is both editor and chief investigative reporter. With a nose to sniff out a story, maybe that is why everyone calls him Snoop?

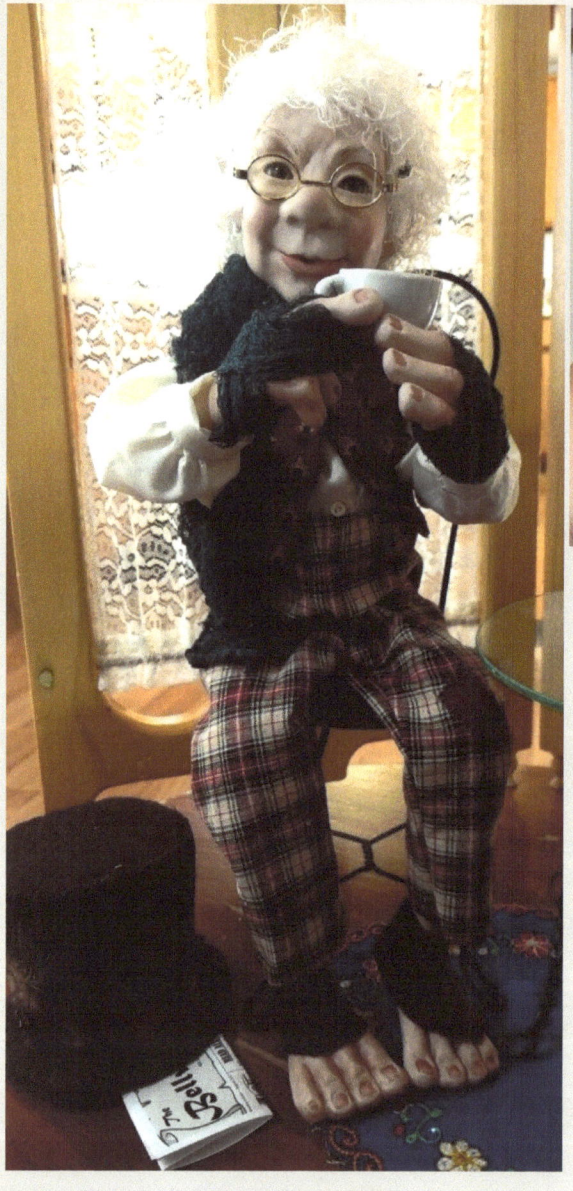

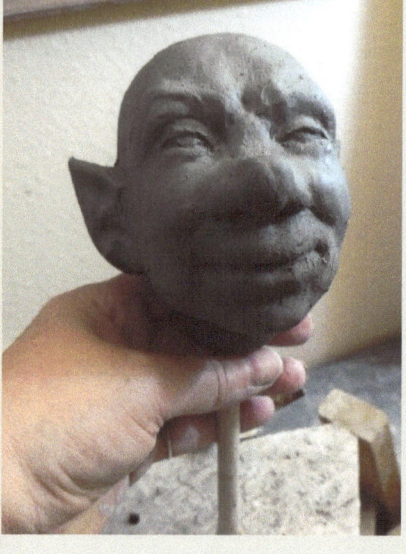

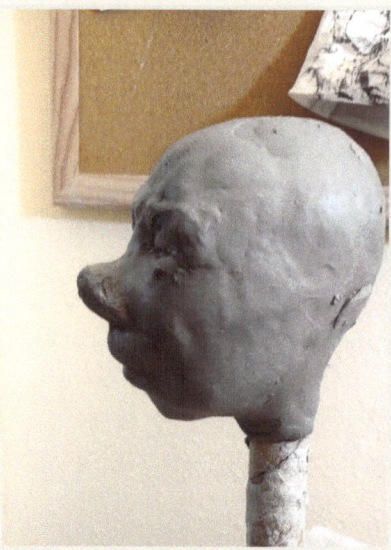

When creating my porcelain dolls the first step begins by Creating the original sculpted head out of a wet clay.

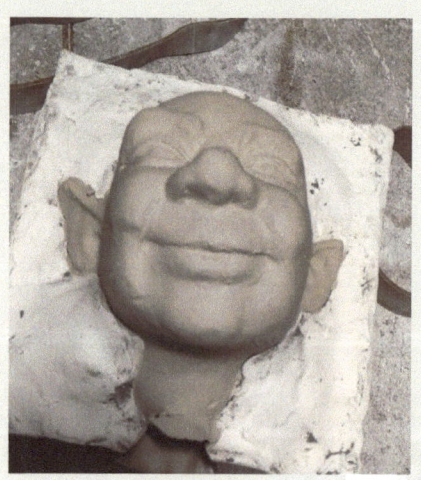

The next stage is making the mold from the clay head. Then pouring the head in porcelain.

MisPlace Dolls

Lesley Duthie
Bigfork, MT

MisPlaceDolls.com

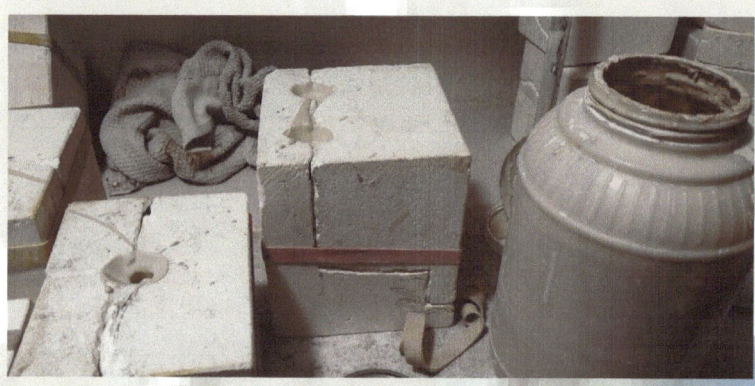

Augustus the Earl of Grey, How an artist made porcelain doll comes to life.
By Leslie Duthie

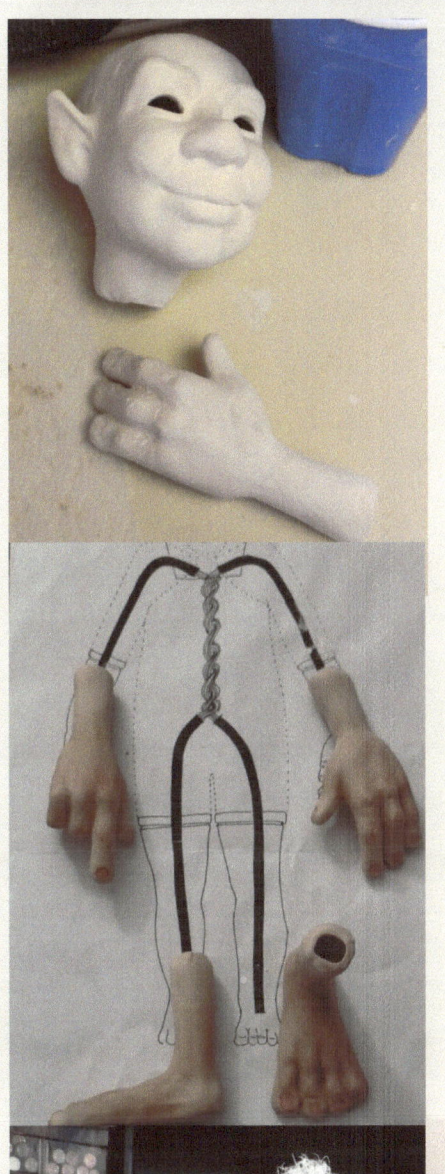

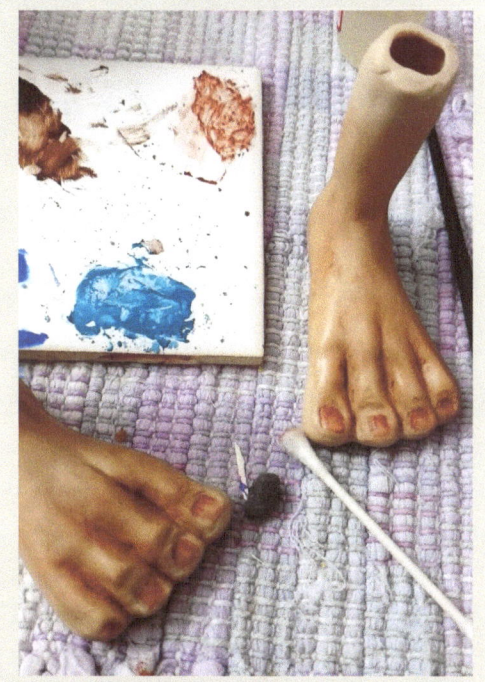

The process after that goes from: the head being in soft fire, cleaned and readied for the final firing.

The picture of the feet.. is the china painting process that also requires another fired on process.

Armature layout for the body which then gets fabricated to the finished body show with him admiring his hat . He loves his hat. lol

After that is the costuming part to the finished doll. Which I make all their costumes . The wigging process is from synthetic fur fabric for

this particular hairstyle.

Contact:

misplacedolls@hotmail.com

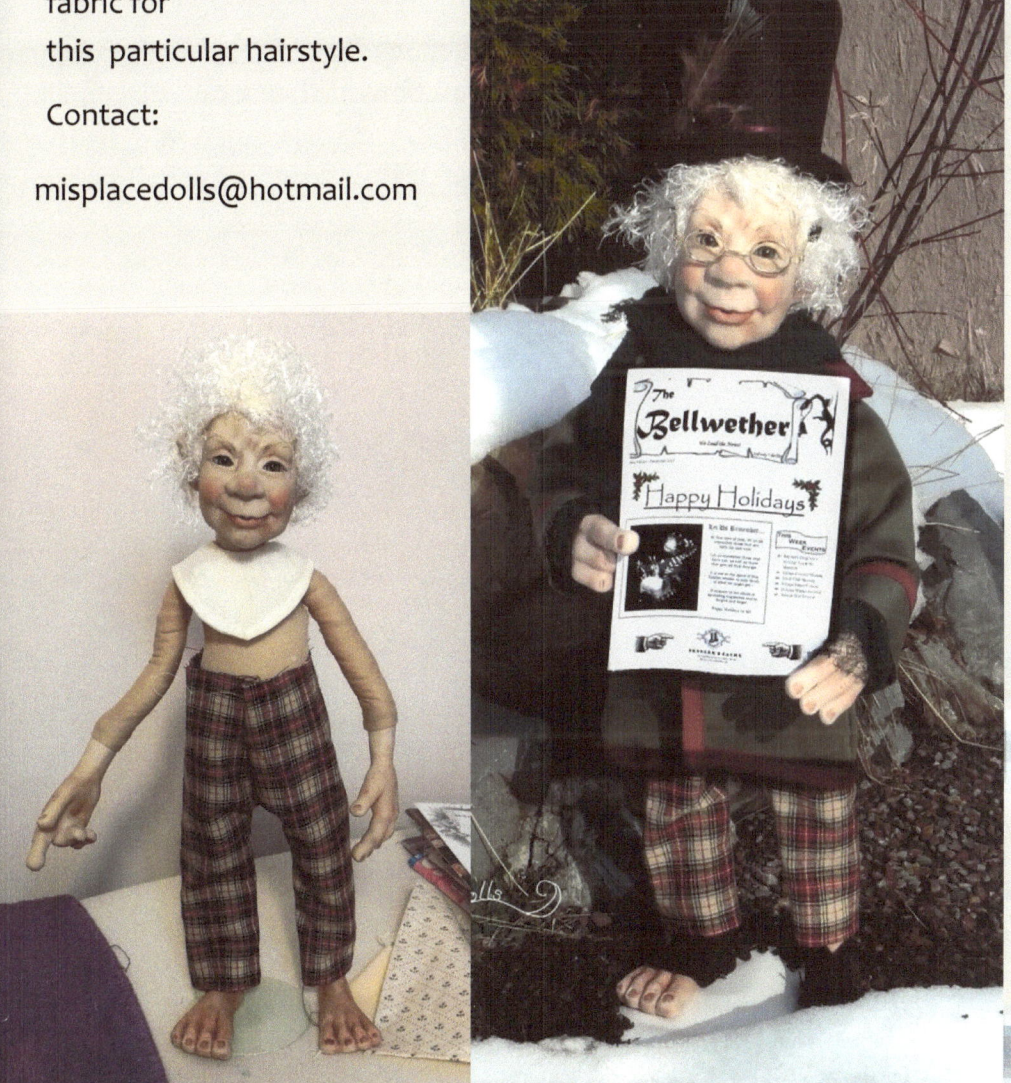

Loving the Historical Costumes
by Elisa Fenoglio

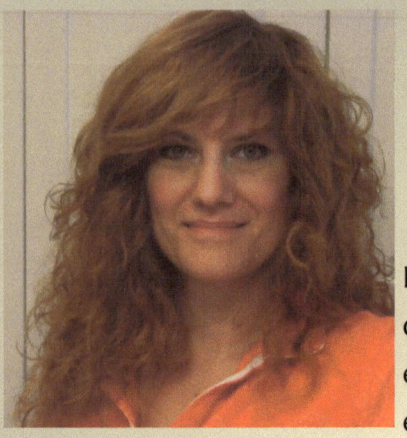

I studied scenography and costume design at the Academy of Fine Arts and ever since my time at university, for my exams, I have had to make models of the scenes and costumes that I invent. A passion was born. Today I continue to invent outfits for my dolls and it is the part that I enjoy most of the whole process. I love recreating antique garments, faithful to their historical periods, preferring those of Georgian and Edwardian.

I love combining materials, laces, ribbons… I look to be as faithful as possible to the period that I am representing while adding a personal touch and often adding more lace than they would have added. For me the best bit of these sculptures is exactly the matching of varied and precious materials. I look for cloths that are similar to those used in the periods I love. Silk brocade for the Georgian period, Superlight silks for the Edwardian. And then the ribbons… thin, again silk, as they reflect the light more, hand dyed and then often retouched so as to match with the colours of the dress material to perfection. The brocades must have very minute patterns so as not to seem disproportionate. The laces have to be antique because they immediately take you back in time. I search amongst the best jewellery artisans for miniature gems and flowers to decorate my dames as best as possible. Sometimes I also personally make flowers and the occasional piece of jewellery out of cloth or synthetic clay.

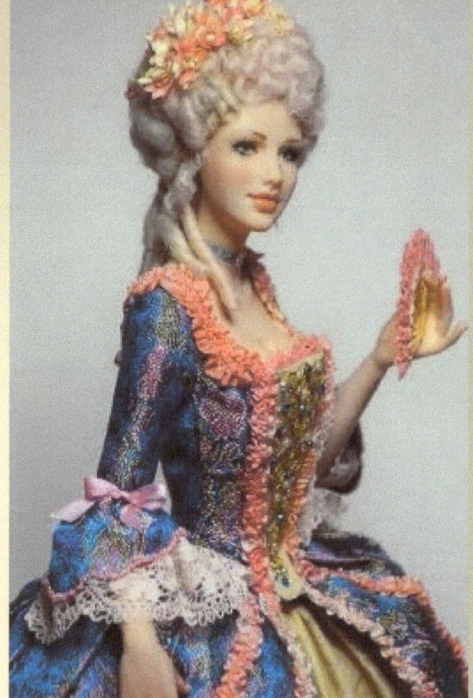

I make dolls in various dimensions, from those in 1:12 scale for dolls houses to larger ones reaching 1:6.

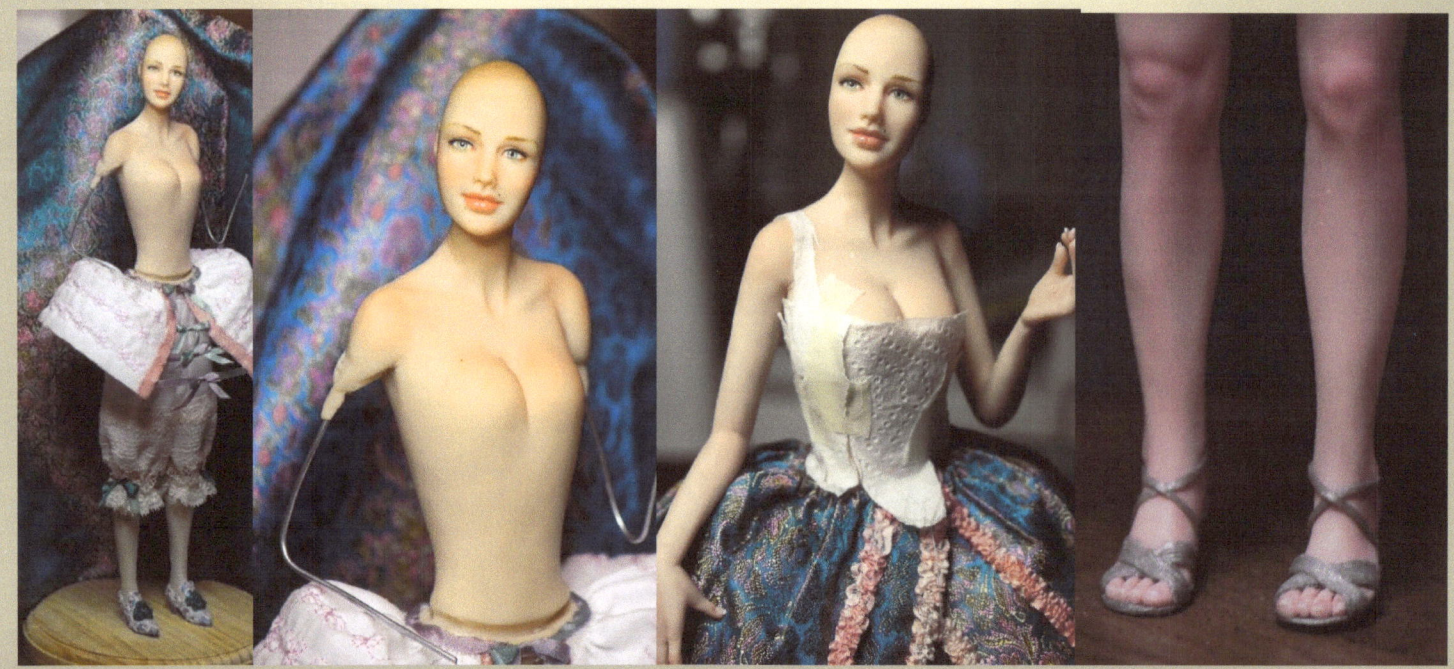

Loving the Historical Costumes

Continued..........

by Elisa Fenoglio

Regarding the clothes patterns, I make my studies in 1:1 scale. I have a few books that I used when I worked in the theatre but I often have to adapt them, removing a few seams or trying to find simpler solutions in order to have a natural effect for such small dimensions.

I always make the underwear for my dolls (panties, petticoats…) even though they won't be seen because I so love making the costumes that they must be complete and at their best.

In order to make a dress for this type of sculpture you must already have the final effect that you want to achieve of the dress in your mind while you are modelling. Sometimes you have to cut the waist a little more so that the skirt will have a more sensual aspect and avoiding seeing excess layers of the skirt which would be unpleasant to see… I don't just make antique costumes though; often I listen to requests of private collectors and try to please them uniting their ideas with a research of traditions and my own personal interpretation. Thus, from the request to make a Geisha, not overdressed, a study of hairstyles, colours and makeup was born… together with a personal interpretation of Japanese undergarments that slightly recall the kimono.

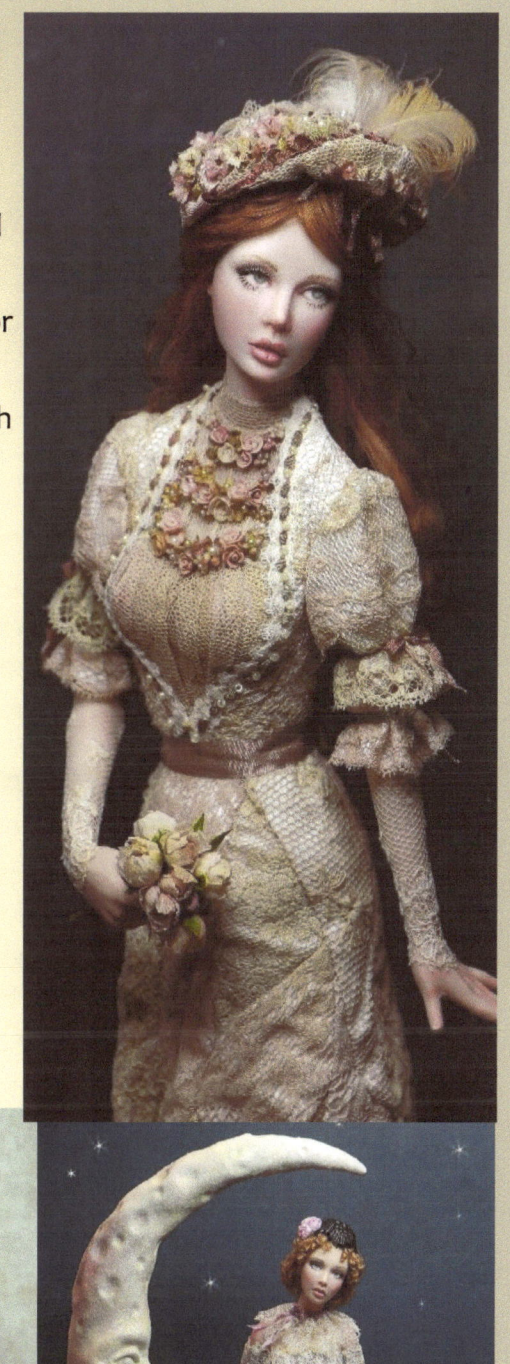

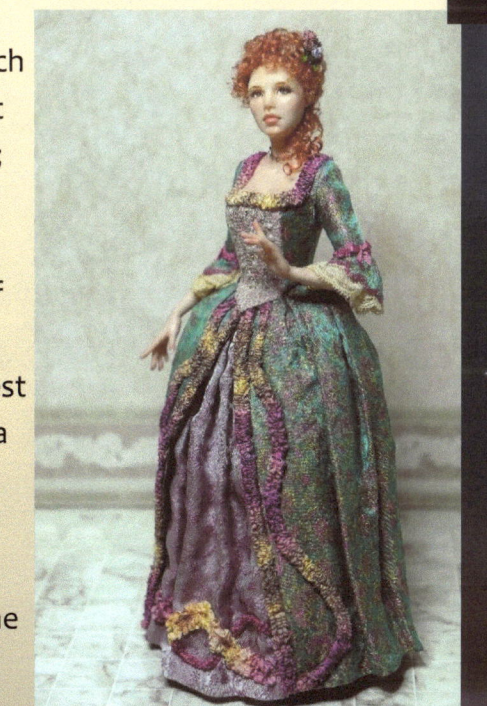

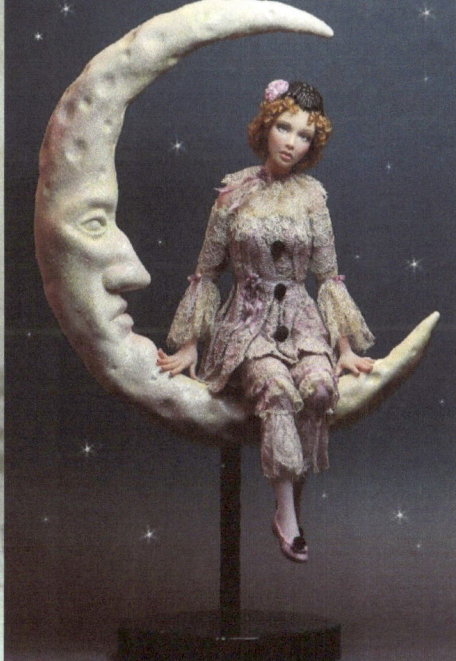

Historical Costumes..........Continued

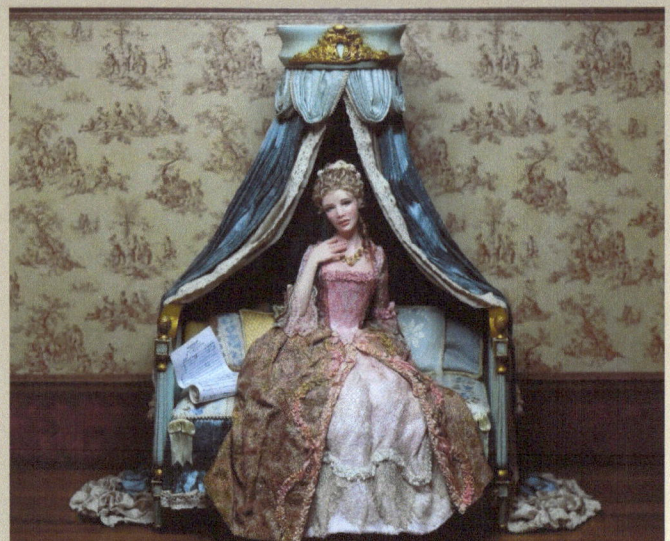

Sometimes I receive requests for wedding portraits: the two dolls to be placed on top of the wedding cake and then be kept as a memento. In these cases, I ask for photos of how the bride and groom will be dressed and I study my modern patterns, trying to make them as realistic as possible on such a small scale.

I have also had fun making some Venice carnival costumes. These are very particular where no part of the body must be left uncovered: people cover their faces with a mask, blacken around their eyes so that no skin can be seen while highlighting the holes in the mask, hands are covered with gloves and the whole costume is an explosion of fantasy from head to toe.

This type of costume can be entirely made-up or related to something specific, such as the seasons, day and night, or any theme that comes to mind. I also greatly enjoy making the costumes for fairies or other characters, personifying them to my own tastes, like the series of Pierrots sitting on the moon that I have made in recent years.

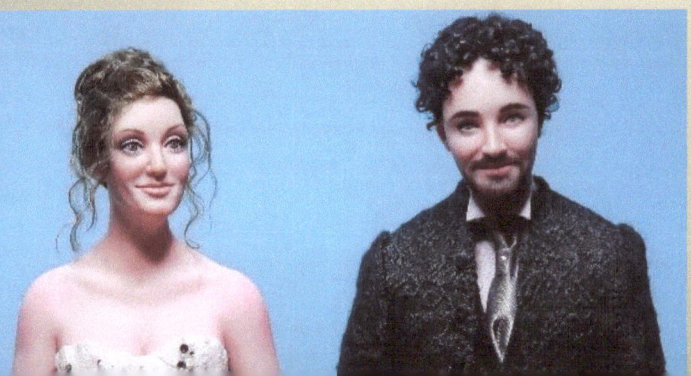

Contact: Elisa.fneoglio@libero.it

Corvus by Sue McMahon

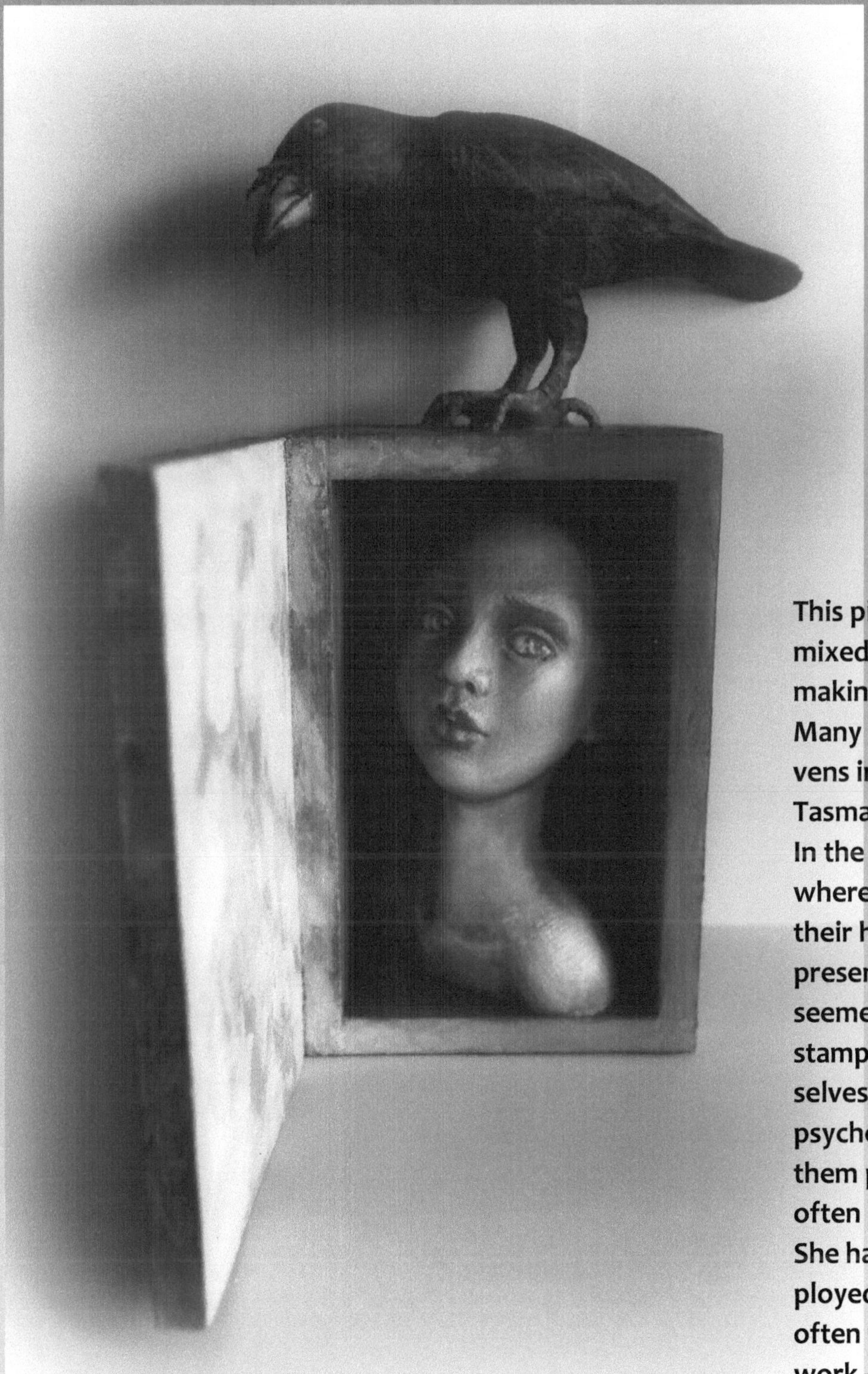

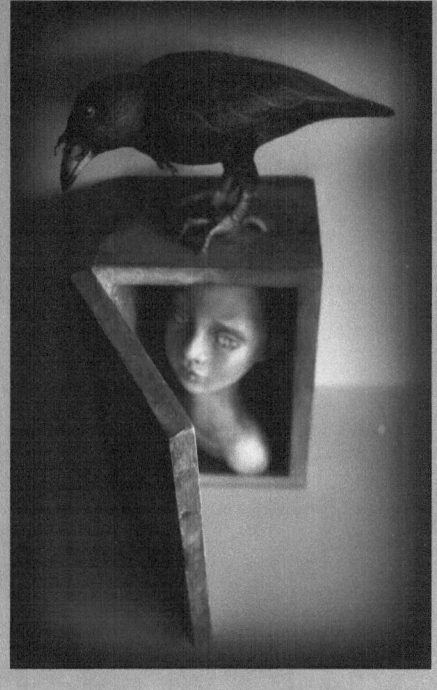

This piece is part of a series of small mixed media works Sue McMahon is making for an up-coming exhibition. Many of the works feature forest ravens in some way - these are native Tasmanian birds of the corvid family. In the isolated and mountainous place where she grew up, these birds, with their haunting call were a ubiquitous presence - they seemed to have stamped themselves onto her psyche, so she finds them popping up often in her work. She has also employed a device she often uses in her work - a box to partially contain the work. This piece is mixed media (wood, air-dry clay, fabric, paint), approximately 12" high painted with artist's acrylics.

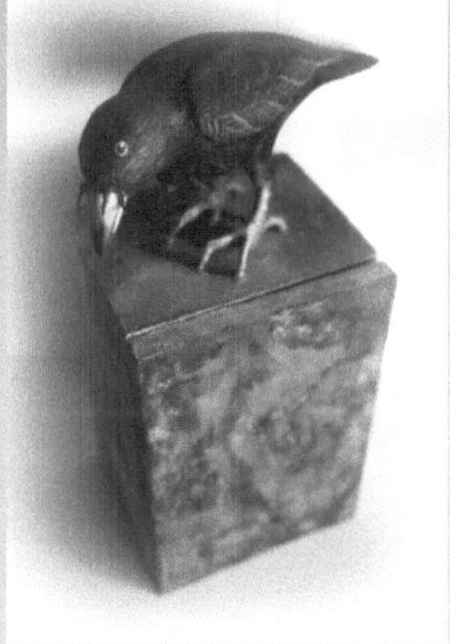

Contact:

Sue McMahon
@launtel.net.au

Creative Costuming

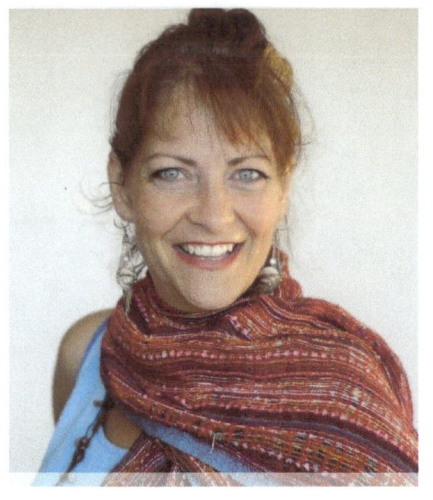

By Rhonda Calhoun

For more than 18 years Rhonda has been involved in costuming – in one form or another – whether in theatre or dressing, this self-taught artist applies a life-time of trial and error including everything she learned beside her Grandmother on her trundle machine. She migrated to doll clothes design and construction for factory dolls for about 2 years, under the name CreamSoda Fashions, before taking on her obvious talent for sculpting and dressing her own dolls.

This award-winning doll artist has recently just completed her 4th BJD sculpt (Stella) and produced outfits for each and every one... to match her personality of curiosity and mischief.

"A lot of times I find inspiration for an outfit in the gently used fabrics of clothing at bazaars or even in my own closet. I enjoy the 'hunt' for unique colors and textures in used clothing (garage sales, thrift stores and my own closet will pique a creation). Who doesn't have those clothes that don't fit anymore, that we've been keeping for 10 years 'just in case'? You probably have some real gems in there! I utilize, in all my designs, a scrap of one, a ruffle from another and something for a pinafore over there….." Nothing is off limits for this creative costumer.

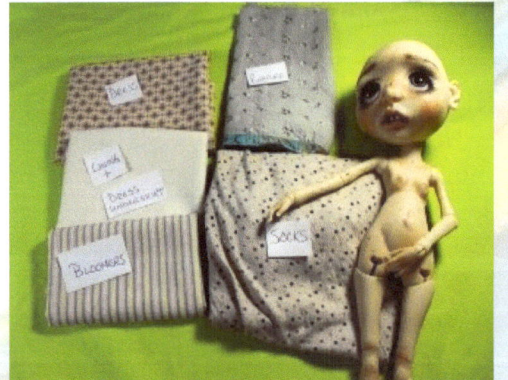
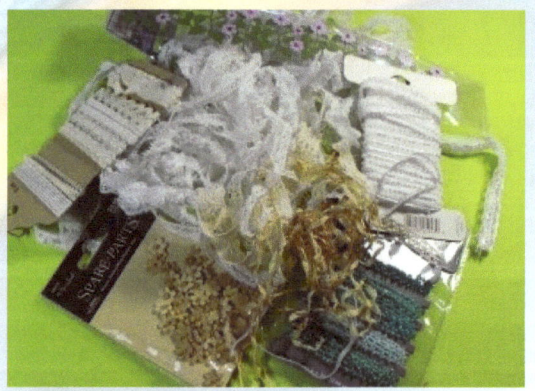

Collect trims from everywhere, fabric shops, dollar stores, removed from used clothing. I almost always tea-dye my doll fabrics so I like to use cottons as well as cotton thread so they will dye nicely. Today I'll be using a mix of new fabrics and trims as well as repurposed cuts from garments.

Lucky model is my latest ball jointed doll (BJD) Stella. She is about 42 cm tall."

"I like to make my initial patterns from paper towels, because they are easy to work with. Once I have them done I transfer the patterns to paper or cardstock which is more durable for repeated use. Be careful not to 'mark' your doll while drawing patterns, for extra protection you can wrap your doll parts in plastic wrap first.

Creative Costuming
Continued

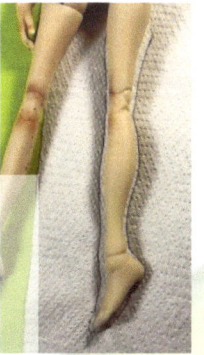

Socks:

Decide how far up the leg you want your sock to come and draw around the entire leg; you will make it about 1/8" – 1/4" wider to allow for a seam allowance. The front part of the pattern will be placed on a fold - so I straighten it with a ruler. Trace your pattern onto paper or cardstock and cut from a stretch fabric with the stretch oriented so it goes 'around' the leg not from the knee to toe.

Mark pattern pieces with part and doll name so there is no guessing later.

I design as I go with no solid plan but feel free to pre-draw your idea or use photos from the internet or other sources.

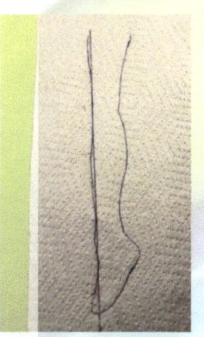

Make a bloomer pattern in the same way as for the socks. Once you have all your pattern pieces. It's easy to adjust leg lengths or necklines, etc. to make different styles by adding a long bloomer pattern to the bottom of a bodice pattern you now have a lovely romper. The bloomers are ready to sew, adding casing for waist elastic and add any trims you would like.

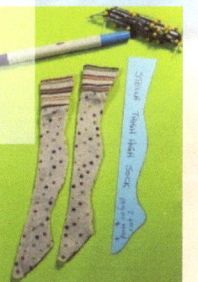

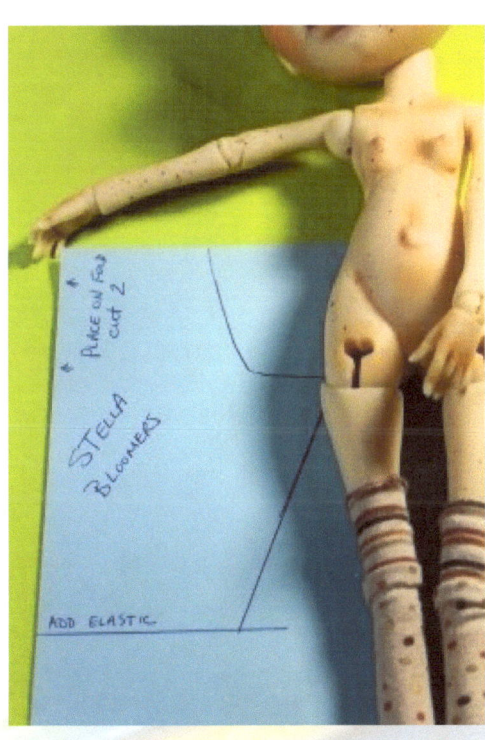
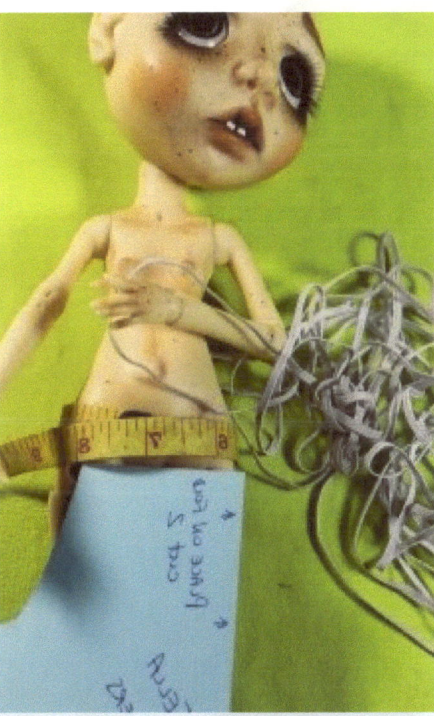
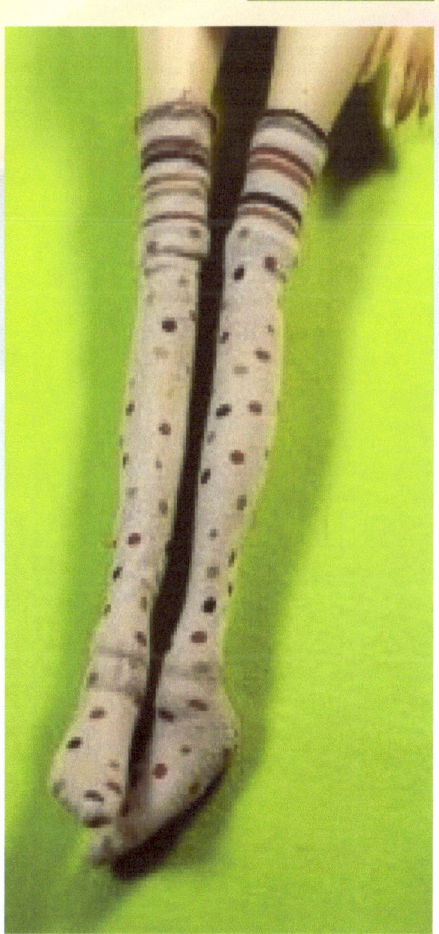
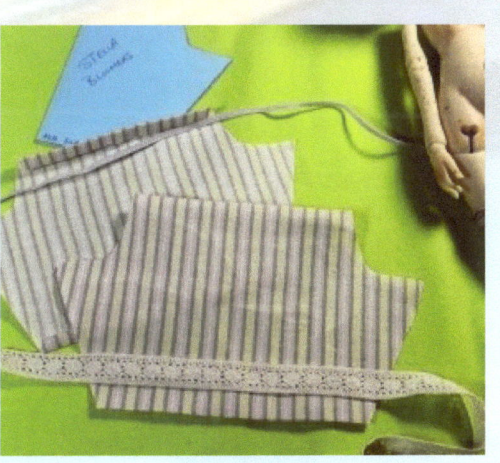
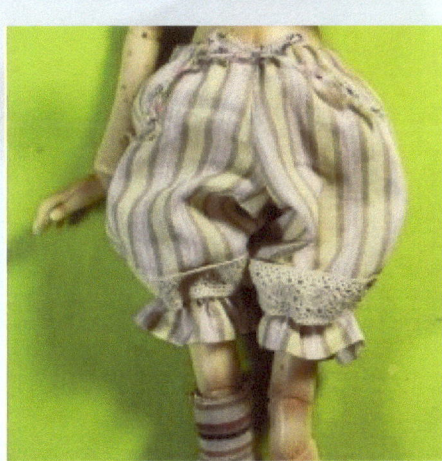

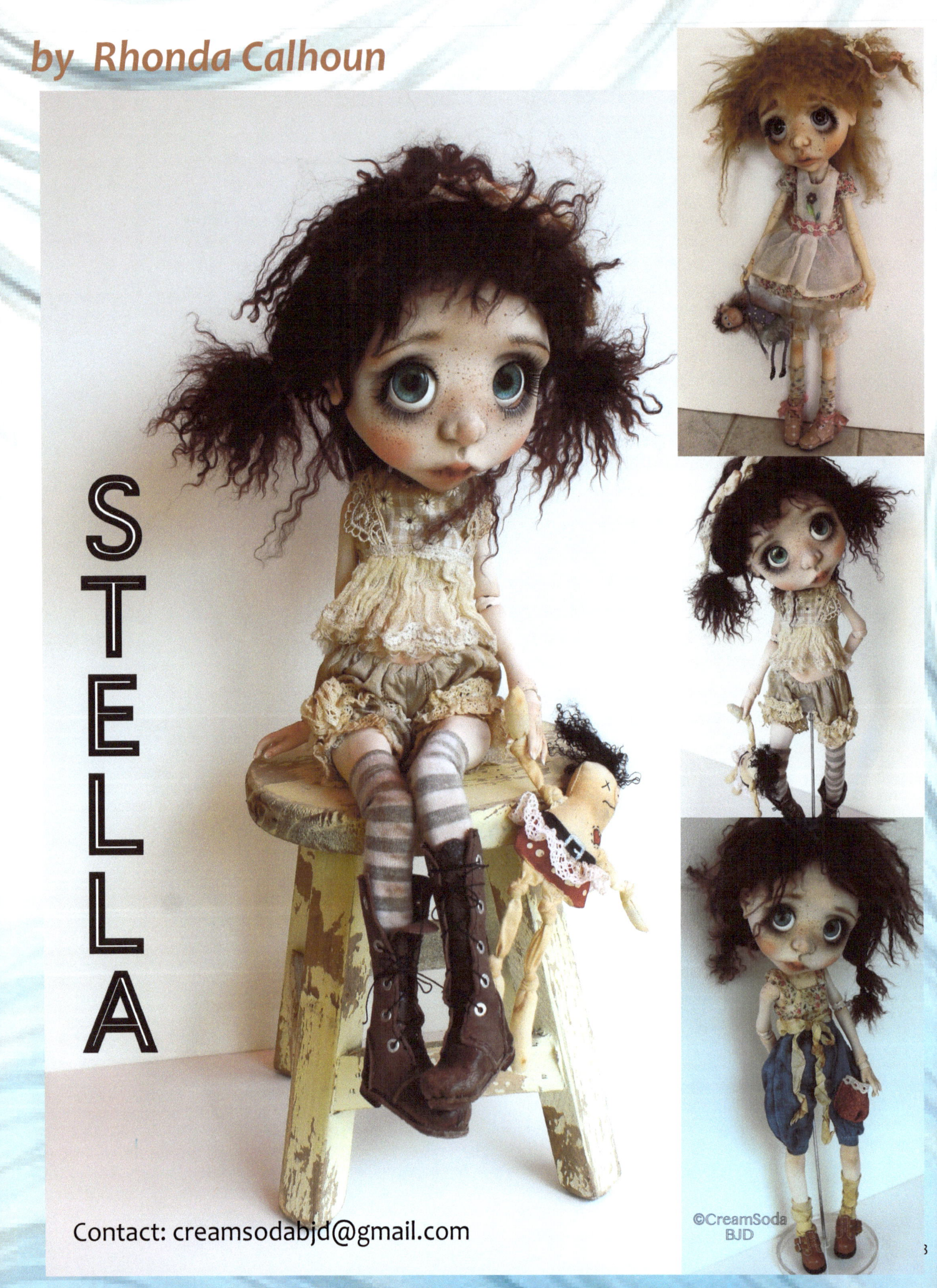

Professional Doll Makers Art Guild Academy

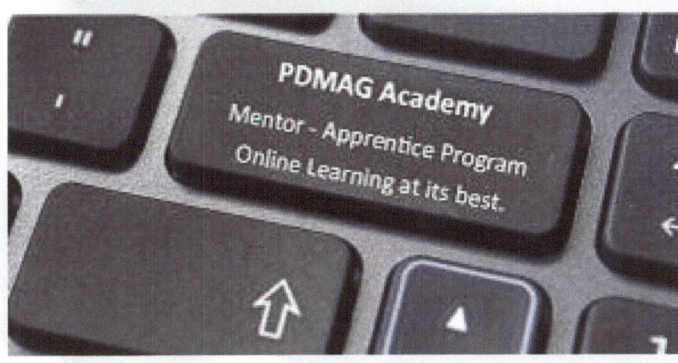

The Apprenticeship program is designed to help Novice artists grow their skills to the level of intermediate or higher so that they may graduate and join the ranks of our artists members and be counted among some the very best art doll creators in the world. Our award winning Master Doll Makers volunteer as mentors so that new and budding artists can learn at an advanced pace to create beautiful art dolls through the PDMAG Mentor/Apprentice Academy.

Come join our mission to help keep this industry going and growing by helping to train the next generation of doll makers and sparking the love of one-of-a-kind art dolls into the next generation.

professionaldollmakers.com

www.artdollguild.com

Contact us at

pdmaguild@gmail.com

Whether you're a Master doll artist who would like to share your skills as a Mentor, or an intermediate artist who would like a little help polishing your work to a more professional level PDMAG can help. We offer guidance into this complex market. If you are a novice artist who wants to learn from the experiences of master doll makers or a complete beginner PDMAG Academy has a place for you.

We now have a Junior sculptors academy which is a multi week program working in our newest group to get newbies up to speed on Polymer clay, armatures, basic anatomy, what supplies you need and then concentrated practice on sculpting your first faces.

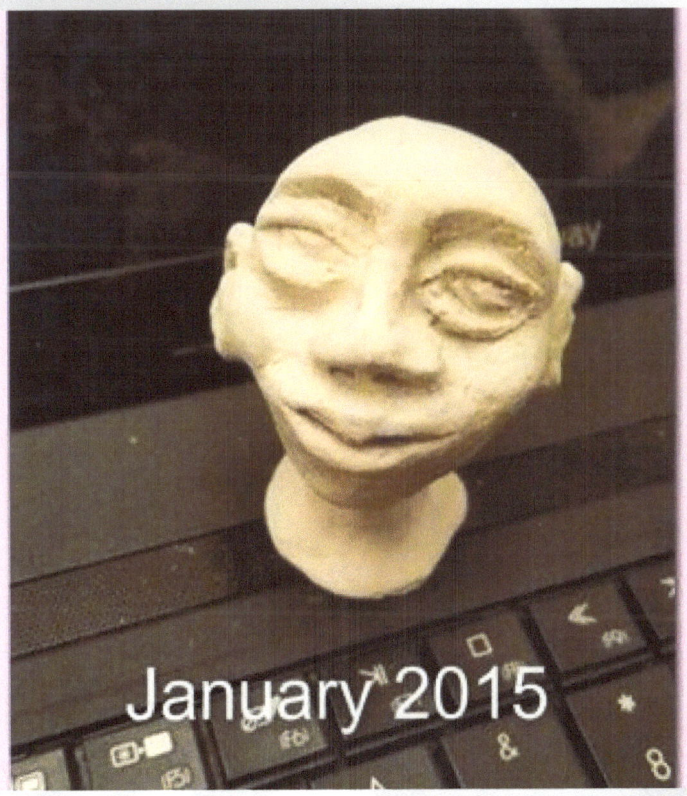
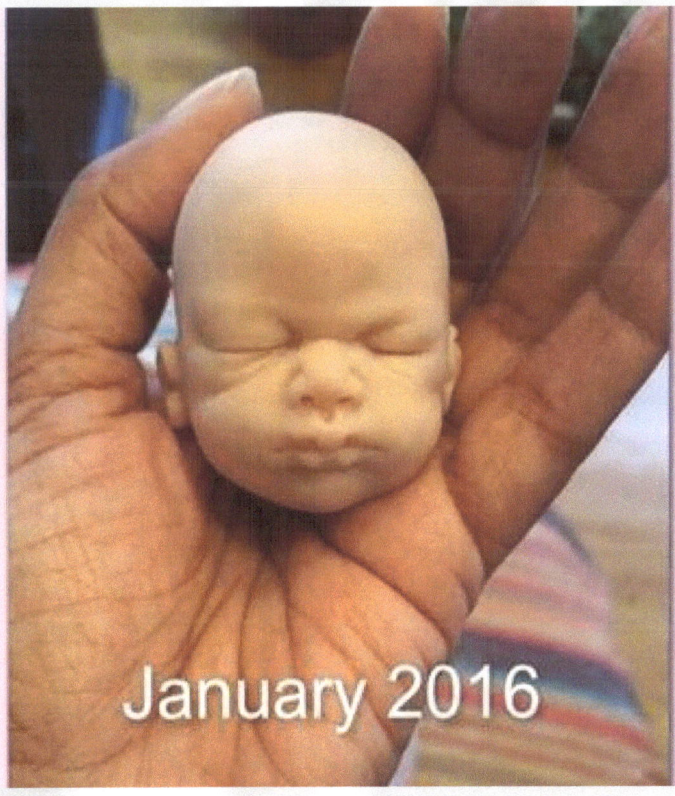

Want to learn at an advanced pace with the help of a professional artist who help you go from I think I can to I know I can. This is a before and after from Apprentice Hope Mason after working with Master Artist Maisa Said for just one year. We have 30 Master artists who volunteer their time to help motivated students learn to sculpt and progress in this wonderful art form.

One piece corset tutorial

by Gayle Wray

Corsets make a real style statement. They've been popular forever and each era has had their own "take" on the shape and style of this versatile garment. It can be worn as outerwear or underwear; either way it's a fashion powerhouse that's here to stay. For this tutorial I've created a one piece design. It's suitable for a young lady because it has a bust minimizing feature. There are no internal stays; it's created by using two layers of fabric with interfacing, or by using two layers of heavier upholstery type fabric, sewn together with reinforcing top stitching. The topstitching mimics the look of the seams around the stays of in a traditional boned corset.

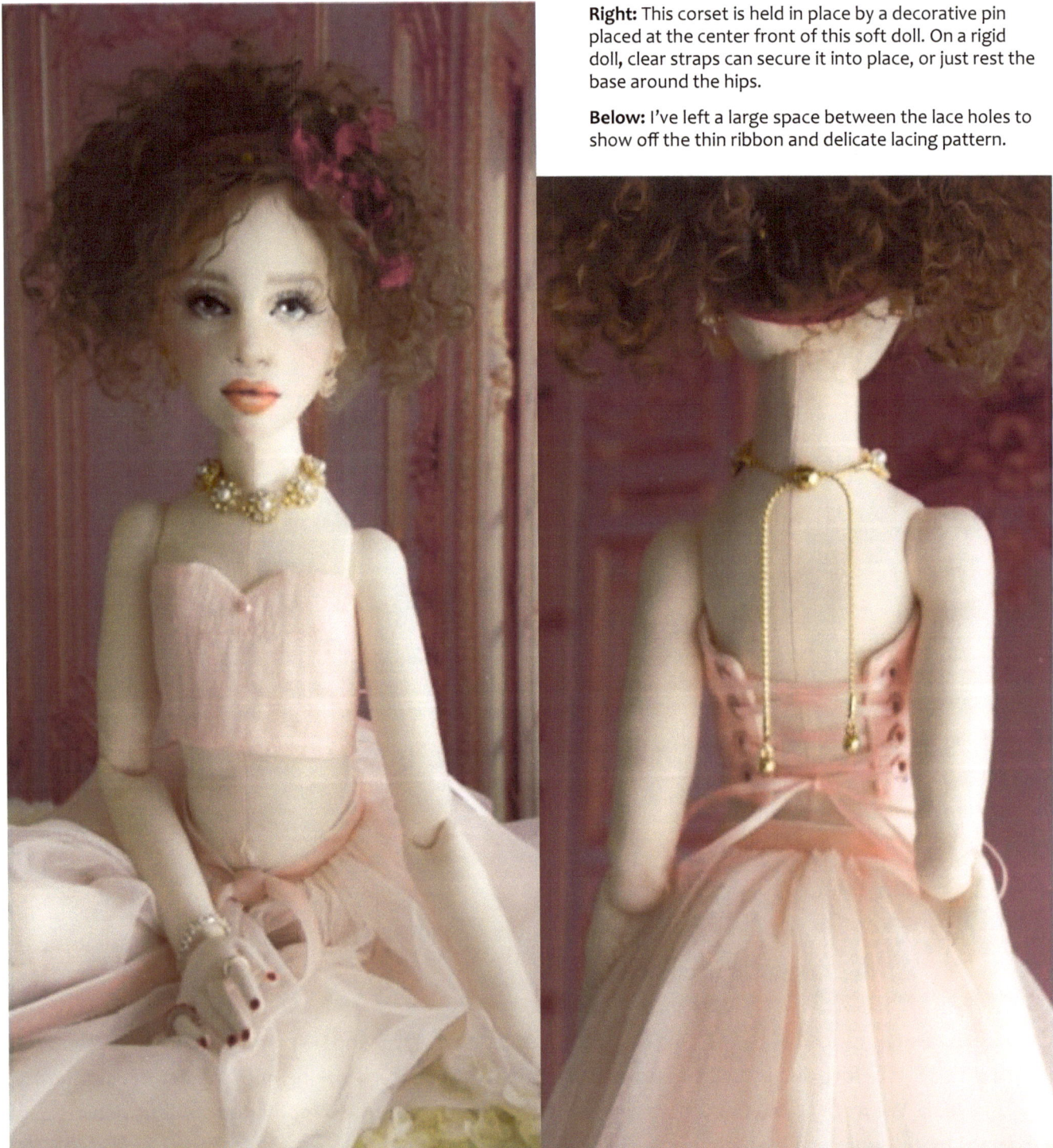

Right: This corset is held in place by a decorative pin placed at the center front of this soft doll. On a rigid doll, clear straps can secure it into place, or just rest the base around the hips.

Below: I've left a large space between the lace holes to show off the thin ribbon and delicate lacing pattern.

Basic corset pattern: Enlarge or decrease it to the size of your doll's bust circumference. Measure your doll across the bust line, keeping the tape level.

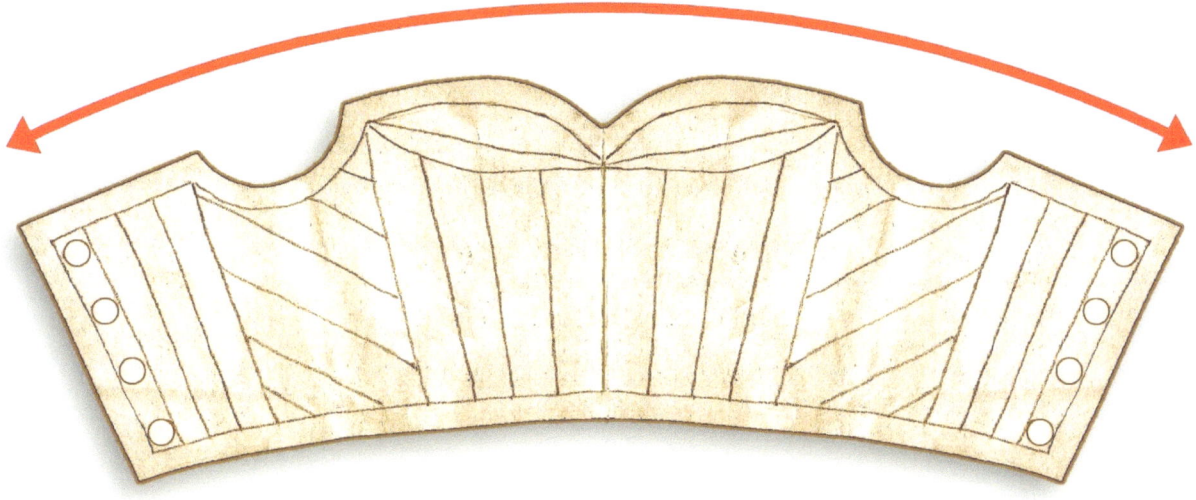

Customize the fit, by tracing this pattern onto copy paper then placing it on your doll to get the best fit from each angle. Continue making one adjustment at a time and with each fix, retrace onto a new paper. Arm cut outs are not mandatory, so omit them if you prefer a straight look across the sides and back. Leave no seam allowance in your template. Trace your pattern onto a thick piece of fusible interfacing. Carefully trim the interfacing and lay it onto the wrong side of your doubled corset fabric and press it into place. Pin the layers of fabric together and sew at a 2.5 stitch length closely around the interfacing, leaving an opening of 1 1/4" at the bottom seam to invert. Trim your corset to within 2/8" and snip the corners. Snip once at the top centered cleavage to allow the sharp turn needed. Reach in with hemostats and turn your corset inside out. Push all edges out gently, tuck the exit seam to the inside, and press the whole corset flat. Add a bit of fabric glue to neatly close the opening.

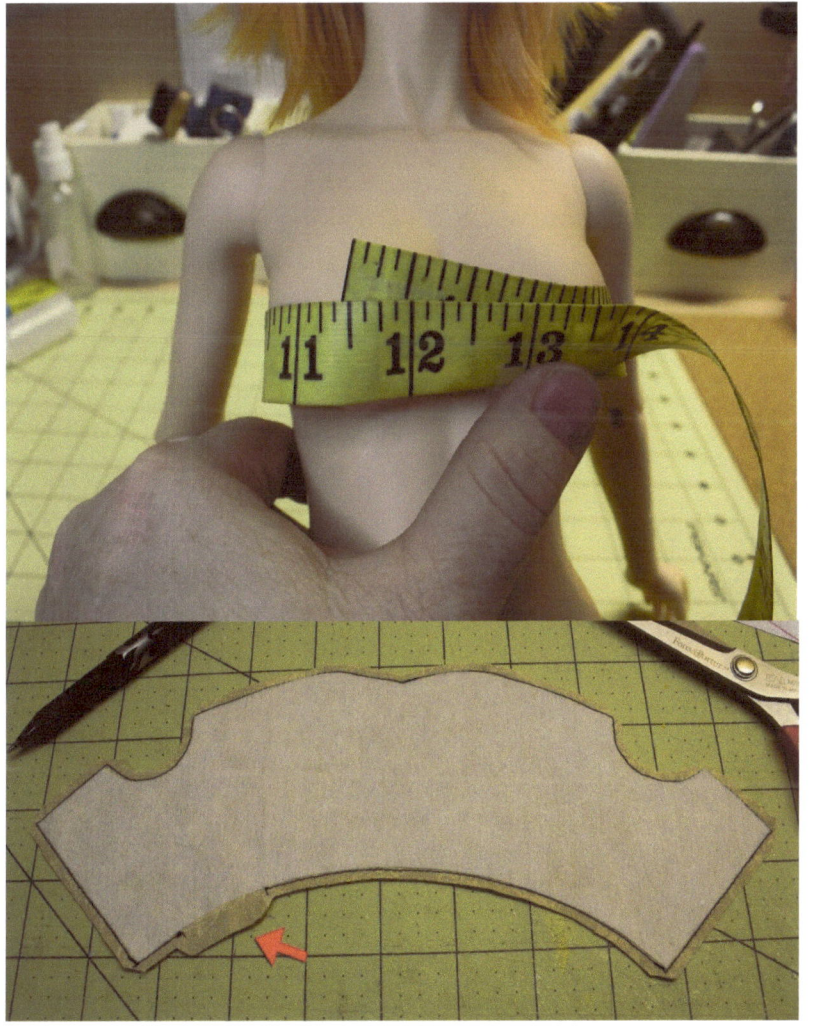

Top stitch pattern:

The lines on the corset patterns are top stitch lines and can be redrawn in any configuration you choose. Take your pattern and draw lines in disappearing ink. Once you've established a nice pattern, transfer it onto your corset front with disappearing ink. You really can't go wrong so be creative and freestyle or follow the lines that I've established. My example below is shown with 2.5 stitch length in contrasting black thread. Sew an initial border around your piece at 1/8". Sew along all your topstitch lines and then press to remove the ink guide lines. I always use a polyester thread because you can melt away all the stray thread ends with cigarette lighter.

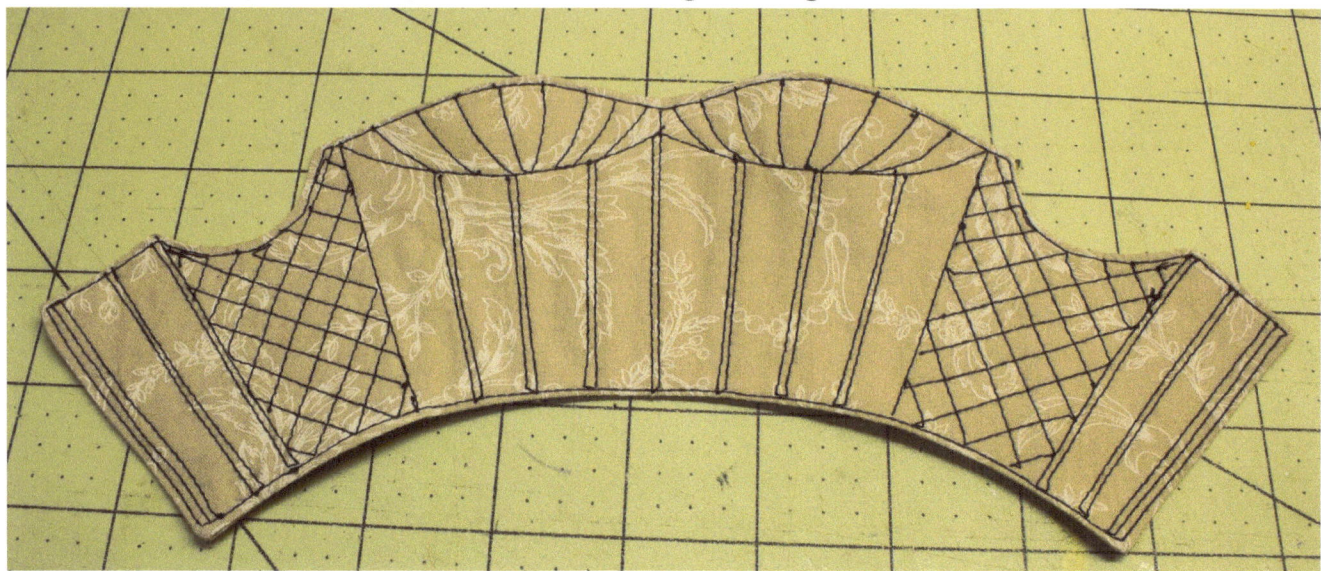

The gap at the back of your corset can be very wide to show more crisscrossing laces, or it can be precise and meet up perfectly with minimal lacing. I've chosen a perfect lineup here. Because the corset is supported by the dolls hips, no straps are needed to keep it in place.

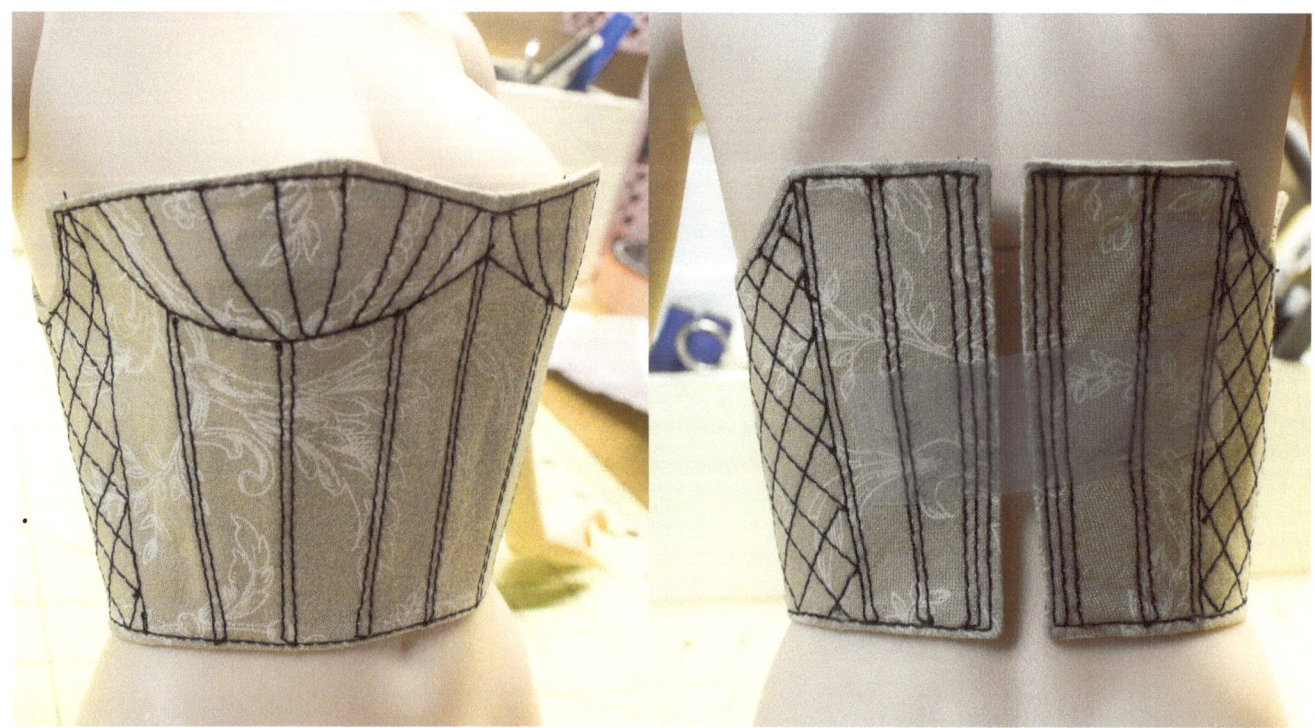

Creating the lace holes:

Laces can be applied in a variety of ways: External exposed hooks from a hook-and-eye set can be sewn on both sides with laces hooked over them, as is done with roller skates. Conversely, the eye part of a hook-and-eye set can be sewn to the inside, so that you can delicately lace with minimal hardware showing. Grommets while tricky do make a nice finish, but the easiest way to lace is to simply create an opening between the threads by gently pushing an awl into the fabric to create a hole. Be careful to not cut the threads. The awl method works best with woven natural fabrics. For this demo, I'll be using the awl method of creating the holes and HugSnug for the laces. I've chosen to make four holes on each side, marked with red dots.

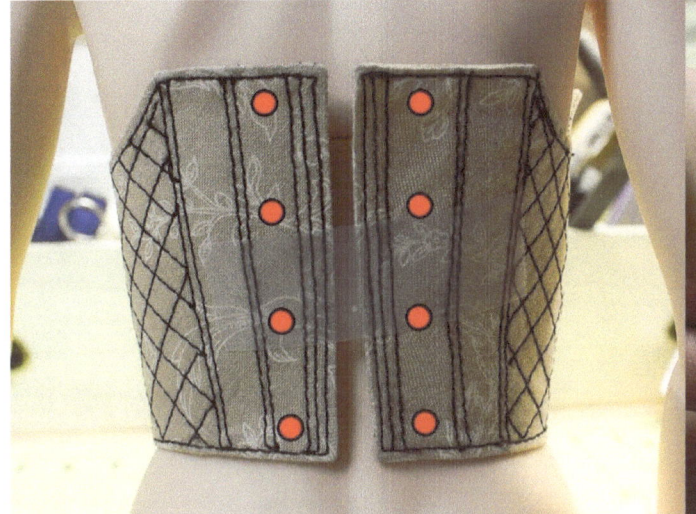

Lacing materials:

Laces can be made of any thin or wide ribbon, but my favorite is Rayon HugSnug or a similar 1/2" rayon seam binding. I like to take a length of about 36", wad it into a ball, and press it with a hot iron. Turn and repeat several times, then crunch the heated ribbon in your palm; rolling it into a ball as it cools to create a crinkly fun lacing material. There are so many ways to lace. Once you've decided on a lacing pattern, thread a chunky yarn needle and pass through the holes twisting if you have to, to make it pass through. Most ribbons are synthetic and can have their ends sealed with a flame. HugSnug is rayon and will not melt, so cut it to length and tie a knot in each end.

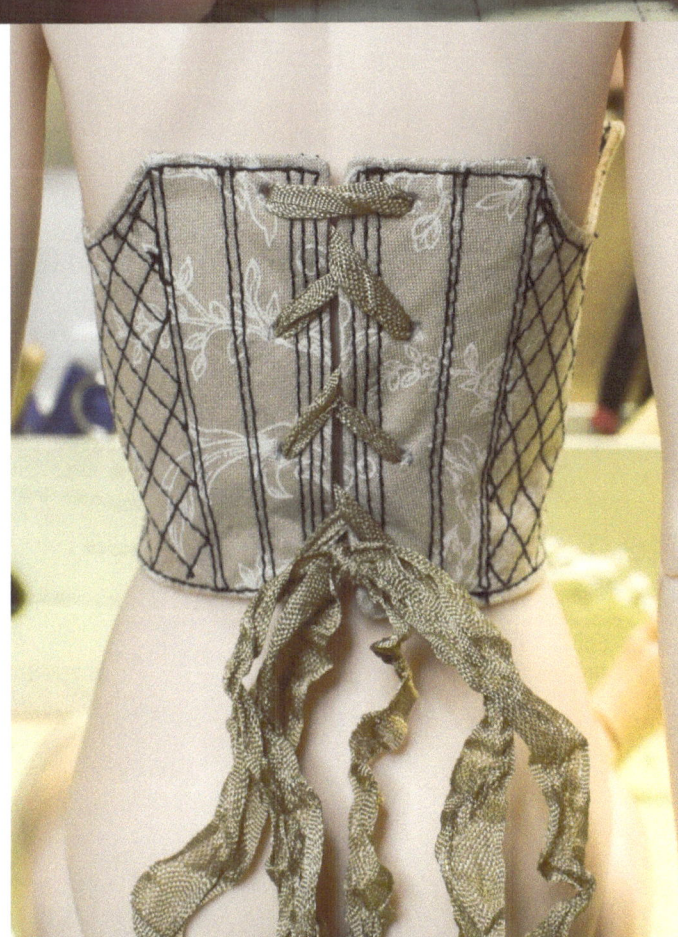

Would you like to learn more about making an articulated cloth doll?

My new book "Making Angelina" is designed as a follow along work book. Each step is illustrated and designed for ease of use. It's a step-by-step guide filled with new techniques and useful hints that will help you create your own fully articulated Angelina doll and outfit!

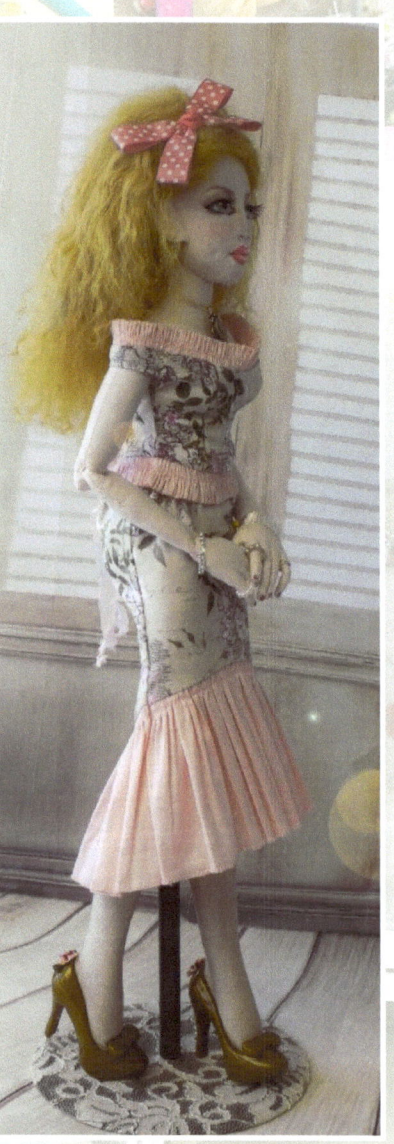

Angelina is a poseable, all-cloth art doll. Like the BJD (ball-jointed-doll) a CJD = (cloth-jointed-doll) is assembled from individually made parts, poseable, and of all cloth construction. She features 10 points of articulation: shoulders, elbows, wrists, hips and knees.

Her measurements are:

- Height 21"
- Bust 8.5"
- Waist 6"
- Hips 10"
- Head 7"

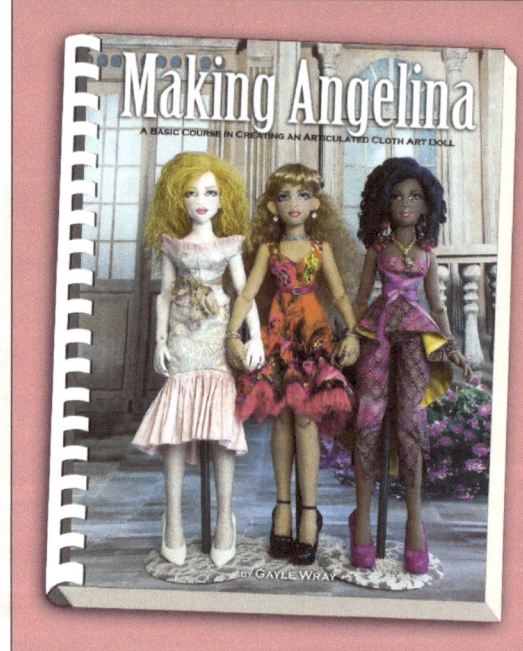

She is an art doll, for adult collectors and not intended to be a child's toy.

Available at http://gaylewraydolls.com

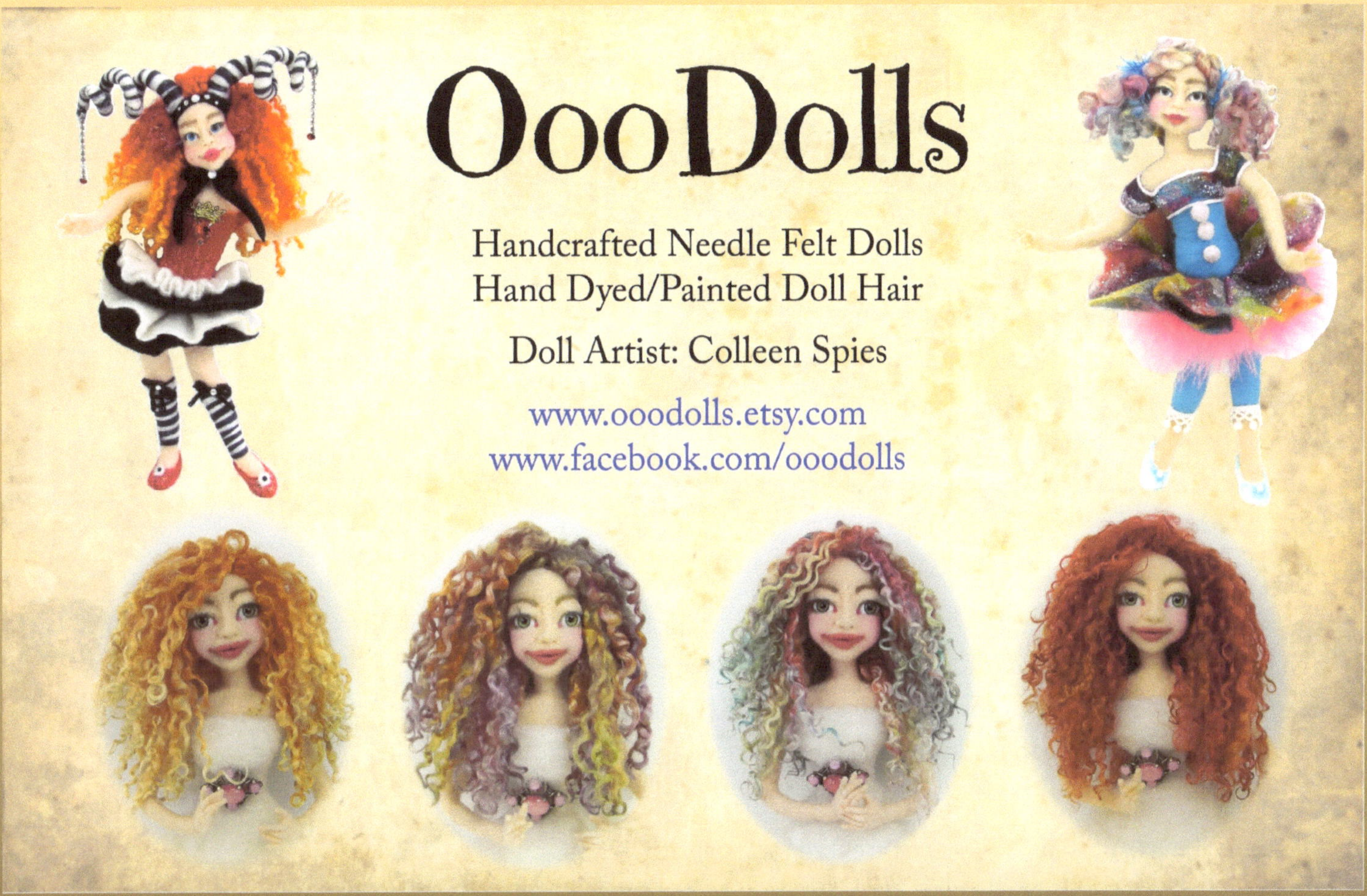

OooDolls

Handcrafted Needle Felt Dolls
Hand Dyed/Painted Doll Hair

Doll Artist: Colleen Spies

www.ooodolls.etsy.com
www.facebook.com/ooodolls

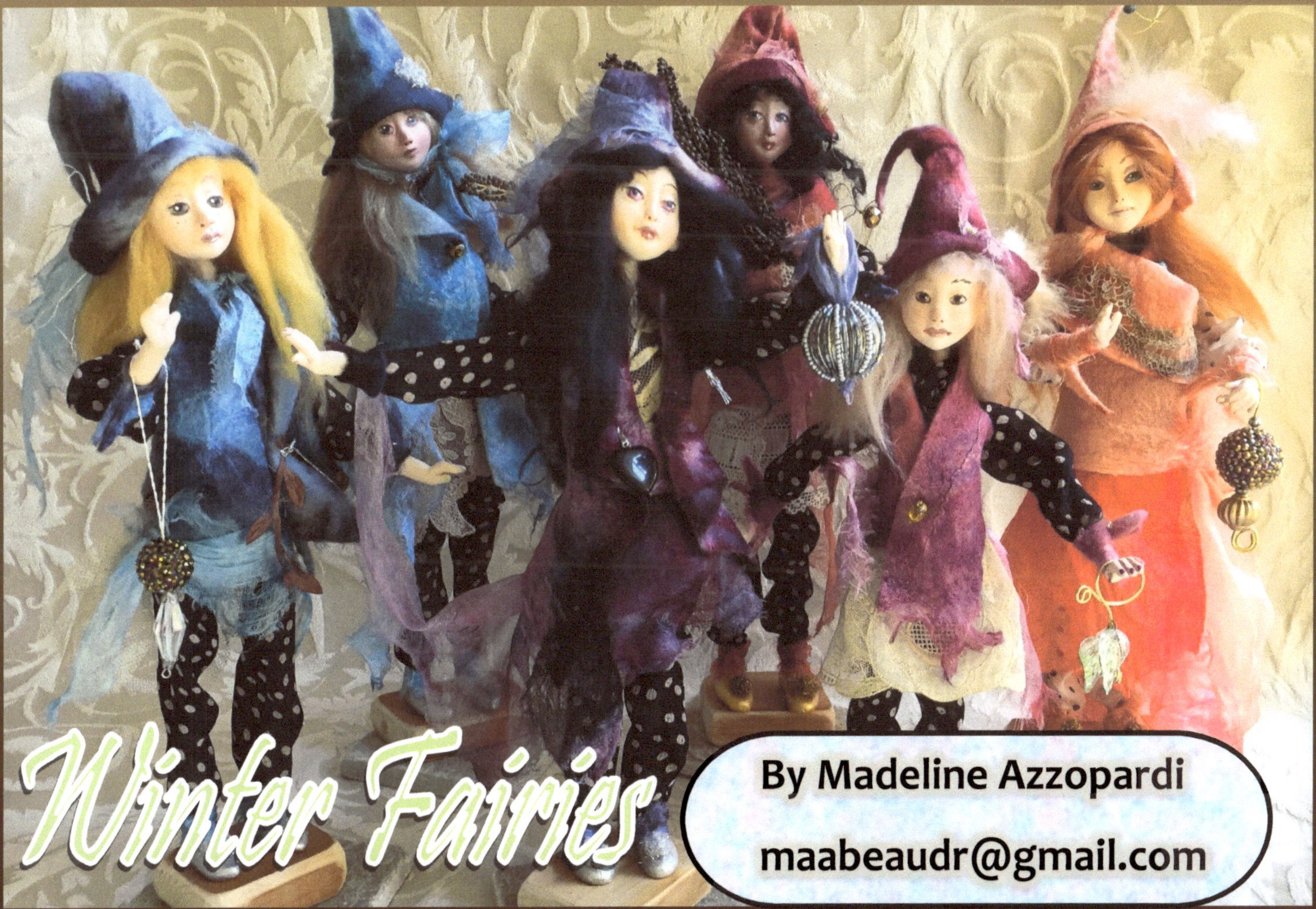

Winter Fairies

By Madeline Azzopardi

maabeaudr@gmail.com

Making Moira's Shoes

By Tami Eveslage

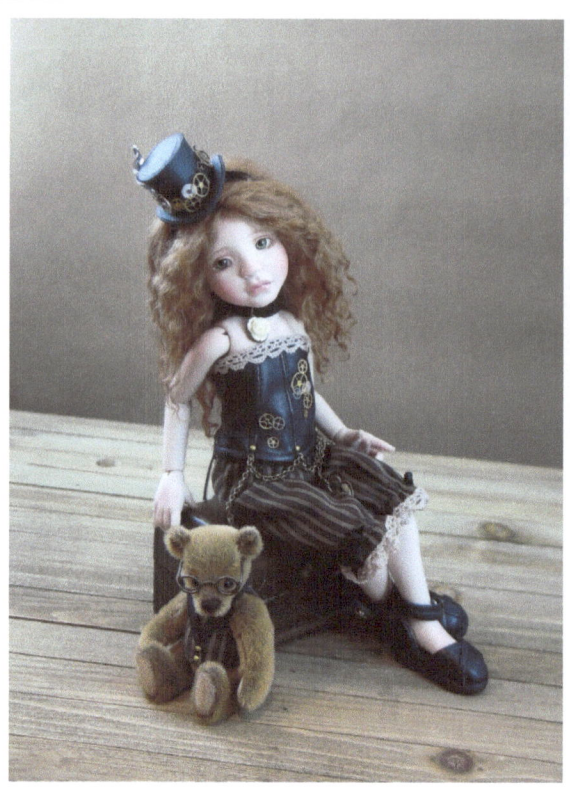

For me, one of the most exciting things about making art dolls is that with each new project, I have a chance to do something I have never done before. Conquering the problem solving exercises involved in making just the right accessory for a doll is such an empowering feeling. I still recall the sheer joy I felt after fashioning my first fabric fungus—a mushroom seat for my Alice doll, the delight I felt looking at the tiny detailed suitcase I made out of my Samsung phone box, and the simple pleasure of carving a pair of toothpicks into diminutive artist's brushes. There is always something new to learn."

This summer, after trying off and on for years, I finally finished my first ball-jointed doll. Unlike the art dolls I have made before with fixed poses and attached clothing, a ball-jointed doll requires removable clothing and accessories. Naturally, I jumped into this challenge feet first!

"Moira and the Professor" is a piece I created for a contest with a Steampunk theme, so when I began to think about Moira's footwear, the obvious choice seemed to be a pair of boots, perhaps a Victorian style with buttons and high heels. However, Moira was supposed to be a little girl, and I had worked so very hard at creating this articulated doll, that I didn't want her to wear anything which would impede the movement of her joints. Consequently, I figured out how to make my first pair of removable Steampunk doll shoes!

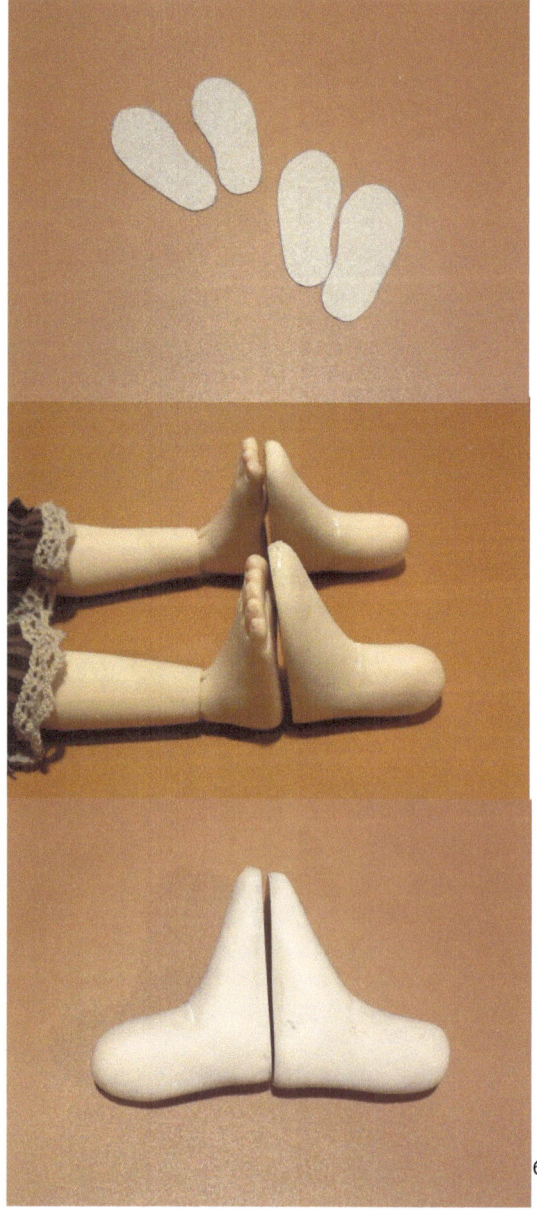

What follows is not so much a tutorial showing how to make doll shoes, as an invitation to learn how I made this particular pair of shoes. I hope it inspires you to do something you have never done before!

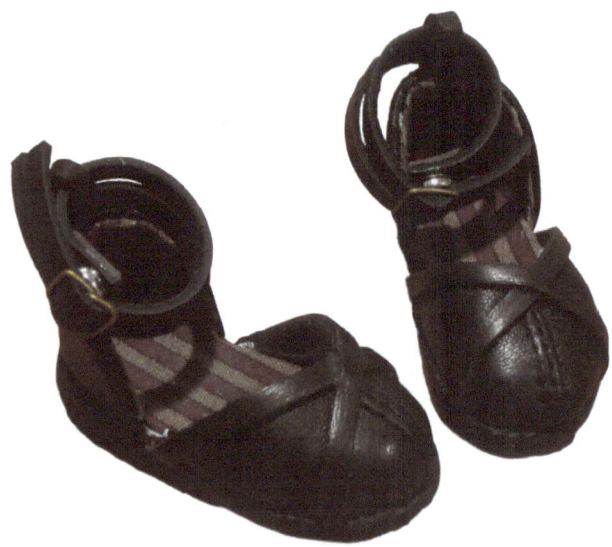

"Making Moira's Shoes" by Tami Eveslage

To make Moira's chunky Steampunk Mary Jane shoes, I began by tracing the dolls bare foot onto cereal box cardboard with a pencil. I rounded out the shape of the toe area by drawing an arch shape just beyond the toes. I cut this sole shape out, and placed it against the bottom of Moira's other foot (reversing it) just to be sure her other foot was a good fit as well. Then I traced it three more times (reversing two) so I had a total of four lightweight cardboard soles. I set one pair aside. Using polymer clay, and one pair of cardboard soles, I created a pair of "shoe lasts", or forms on which to build the shoes. With Moira's feet as reference, I sculpted two simple rounded-toe boot shapes, a left and a right, over a core of aluminum foil. I sculpted these directly onto the cardboard soles, taking care to match the height and width of Moira's feet. I found that placing the sole of the shoe last against the sole of Moira's bare foot and comparing from all angles was a useful way to do this. Using this sole to sole comparison method also helped make certain that the shoe lasts matched each other. I baked the polymer clay to cure it and pealed the cardboard soles off and discarded them.

Next, I made the inner soles of the shoes. I painted one side of each of the remaining cardboard soles with a thin layer of Mod Podge and placed them on the wrong side of a piece of lightweight cotton print fabric I had chosen for the lining of the shoe. When the glue dried, I cut out them out of the fabric leaving a scant quarter of an inch all the way around each sole. Using small sharp scissors, I cut tiny v-shaped notches all the way around each one, and then I folded the excess fabric and glued it to the back.

Then I created the back of Moira's shoes. Using the lightweight cardstock of an index card, I cut a (roughly) semicircular piece to become the back of the shoe. I checked the size against the shoe last. I wanted the straight line to be flush with the bottom edge of the shoe last, and to wrap all the way around the heel. When I had the size and shape I wanted, and it was symmetrical, I traced it to cut out three more, again making two pairs. I covered one pair of these in the same lining fabric I used for the soles, following the same procedure. The other pair of cardstock heel backs was covered with leather from a black glove which had lost its mate, and the leather heel back, beginning at the bottom of the leather and the leaving more than enough extra at the top to make the loop. Then I poked two holes with the point of an awl all the way through the deerskin, the leather, and the cardstock, and inserted tiny brass brads into them, opening the tines flat on the cardstock side to lock them in place. Bringing the loose end of the lace around to the cardstock side, and gluing it into place, I created a loop just big enough to accommodate two widths of straps.

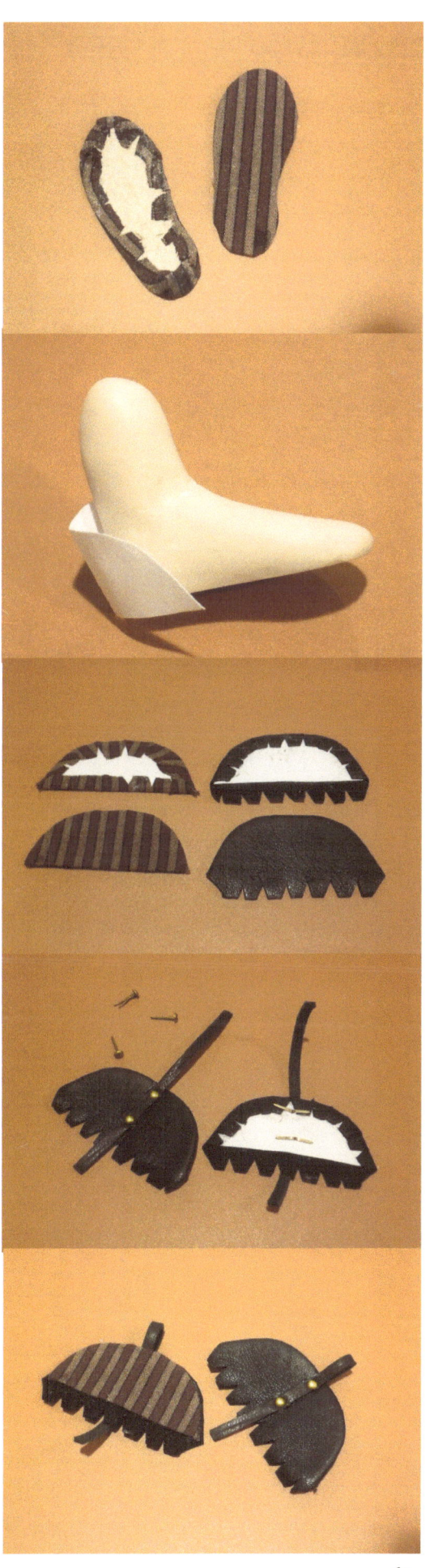

"Making Moira's Shoes" by Tami Eveslage

Finally, I spread a layer of the Fabritac glue to the cardstock side of the leather heel back and pressed the fabric covered piece over it, sandwiching the short end of the loop between the pieces, and making sure that the rounded edges matched up. I cut v-shaped notches in the exposed leather along the bottom. I repeated each step with the other shoe.

It was time to make the front of the shoes. Using dampened buckram, a coarse fabric which can be shaped when wet, I wrapped the front of each shoe last, stretching it slightly, and smoothing out any lumps or folds. I gathered the excess fabric at the bottom of the shoe and clipped it with a binder clip until it was dry. When it was dry, I slid it off of the shoe last, and cut away the bulk of extra fabric at the bottom, leaving about a quarter of an inch of the buckram to wrap around the underside. Next, I slid the stiff buckram form back onto the shoe last, and used a pencil to draw a line indicating how high on the foot I wanted her shoes. I slid it back off to cut on the line. I then placed the fabric covered sole against the bottom the shoe last with the fabric side against it. Holding the sole in place, I slid the buckram piece back on and glued the edges to the bottom of the sole forming something like a house slipper. While it was still on the shoe last, I spread a layer of Fabritac over the buckram and laid a piece of glove leather over it stretching it slightly to make it smooth. The glove I found had some nice top stitching which I took advantage of by placing it so it created a seam down the front of the shoe. I cut way the excess leather leaving just enough to wrap and glue to the underside of the sole. I did this, notching as needed to avoid bulk. I used more of the deerskin lacing to create a cross pattern for a nice design element and to finish the ledge of the leather. It was glued in place using Fabritac, folding the ends under the sole.

I put the shoe backs on next. With the leather "house slipper" still on the shoe last, I bent the shoe back around the heel and glue the notched leather to the underside of the sole. The procedure was a little different. For the outside heel back, I spread a thin layer of Fabritac glue on one side of the cardstock semicircle and placed it on the back of the leather. I cut around the shape leaving a scant quarter of an inch around the arched side and slightly more along the straight edge. Then, on the curved part only, I cut the notches to fold over and glue the leather to the wrong side with Fabritac. The extra leather along the straight edge of the heel back remained exposed at this point. Before attaching the leather and the lining pieces of the heel backs together, I considered how the straps would be attached. I had some flat, lightweight, deerskin lacing I planned to use for the straps. It was 1/8th of an inch wide, and I planned to make a double strap for interest. I decided that creating a loop with the lacing was the best way to affix the straps to the shoes. To do this, I glued a length of the lacing (using Fabritac again) in a vertical line to the outside of the shoe.

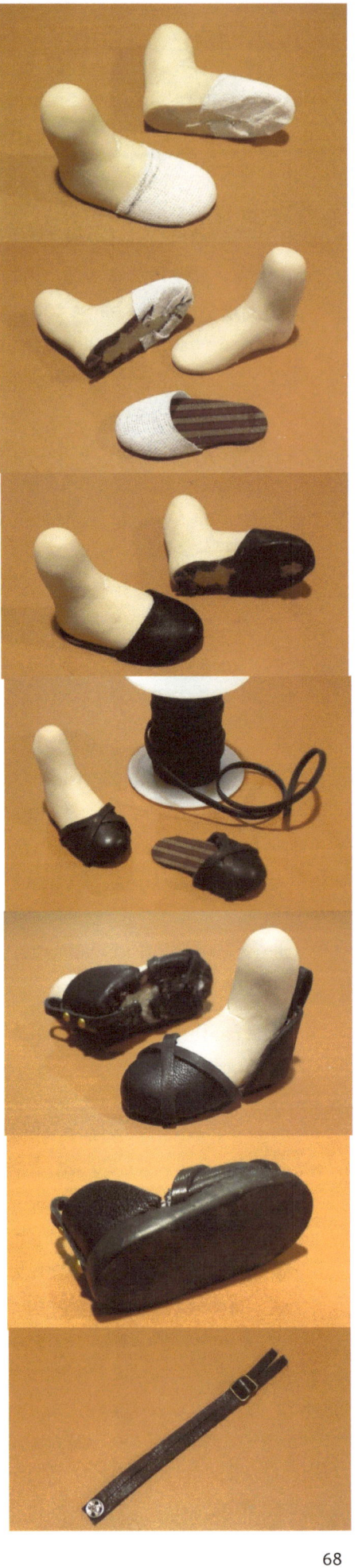

"Making Moira's Shoes" by Tami Eveslage

In spite of trying at each step to eliminate as much bulk as possible, the bottom of Moira's shoes were quite lumpy at this point, and simply adding a cardboard or leather sole on top of that would not work. I mixed up some black Apoxie Sculpt intending to fill in the gaps and even things out, when it occurred to me that I could simply use that material to make the soles! To do this, I first filled in the gaps with small bits until the underside was fairly flat. Then, I gently pressed the shoes only a sheet of the clay I had rolled out. I cut around the shoes with a scalpel, refined the edges and let the Apoxie Sculpt cure.

The final task in making Moira's shoes was to make the straps. For each shoe, I cut two lengths of the deerskin lacing long enough to go around her ankles with about 5/8th of an inch of overlap. I fashioned a decorative buckle by bending a jewelry headpin into my desired shape. I threaded the two straps side by side into the buckle and used an epoxy glue to attach one side of a small snap fastener behind the buckle. On the opposite end of the straps, on the back side, I glued a tiny strip of leather to hold the two straps together. On the front side I glue the other half of the snap.

Supplies:

Thin cardboard, Index card, Unwanted glove or glove leather, Lightweight flat lacing such as deerskin 1/8th inch wide, Lightweight cotton fabric (for shoe lining), Mod Podge, Fabritac Glue, Apoxie Sculpt, Buckram

Contact: tamieveslage@gmail.com

THE ANGEL DOLL COMPANY

- Learn to Sculpt
- Reborn Babies
- Doll Kits
- Paint A Friend
- Collectibles
- Silicone Doll Art
- OOAK Dolls
- Special Events
- Birthday Parties

45 N. Market St.
Lancaster, Pa 17603
717-947-4328
theangeldollcompany@gmail.com

www.ingramcontent.com/pod-product-compliance
Lightning Source LLC
Chambersburg PA
CBHW051202220526
45473CB00003B/869